30 Day Anti Inflammatory Diet Challenge

Anti Inflammatory Diet Cookbook to Heal Your Immune System and Restore Your Health in Only 30 Days

Ellie Silver

Legal notice

This book is copyright (c) 2017 by Ellie Silver. All rights are reserved. This book may not be duplicated or copied, either in whole or in part, via any means including any electronic form of duplication such as recording or transcription. The contents of this book may not be transmitted, stored in any retrieval system, or copied in any other manner regardless of whether use is public or private without express prior permission of the publisher.

This book provides information only. The author does not offer any specific advice, including medical advice, nor does the author suggest the reader or any other person engage in any particular course of conduct in any specific situation. This book is not intended to be used as a substitute for any professional advice, medical or of any other variety. The reader accepts sole responsibility for how he or she uses the information contained in this book. Under no circumstances will the publisher or the author be held liable for damages of any kind arising either directly or indirectly from any information contained in this book.

Table of Contents

Key Facts about the Anti-Inflammatory Diet 14

How Will This Diet Help Me? 15

How Is Food a Factor in Preventing Inflammation? 15

So Which Foods Are Considered Anti-Inflammatory? 16

    1) Fish with Plenty of Fatty Acids 16

    2) Veggies 16

    3) Nuts 16

    4) Beans and Legumes 17

    5) Fruit 17

    6) "Good" Fats 17

    7) Whole Grains 17

    8) Mushrooms 17

    9) Condiments (Herbs) 18

Top 5 Foods that Fight Against Inflammation 18

    1) Salmon 18

    2) Olive Oil 18

    3) "Greens" 18

    4) Berries 18

    5) Turmeric 18

Top 5 Foods You Should Completely Avoid 19

    1) Sugar 19

    2) Cooking Oils (that Aren't Olive) 19

    3) Trans Fats 19

- 4) Red Meat 19
- 5) Refined Grains 19

Day 1: Breakfast 20

1-Healthy Overnight Oats 20

Day 1: Lunch 22

2-Warm Turmeric Carrot Soup 22

Day 1: Dinner 24

3-Yummy Tomato Turmeric Soup 24

Day 2: Breakfast 26

4-Delicious Apple Cinnamon Quinoa 26

Day 2: Lunch 28

5-Slow Cooker Broccoli Turmeric Soup 28

Day 2: Dinner 30

6-Zucchini Avocado Broccoli Salad 30

Day 3: Breakfast 32

7-Anti-Inflammatory Chia Turmeric Pudding 32

Day 3: Lunch 34

8-Refrshing Cucumber Salad 34

Day 3: Dinner 36

9-Tasty Lentil Quinoa Curry 36

Day 4: Breakfast 38

10-Mango Yogurt Overnight Oats 38

Day 4: Lunch 40

11-Easy Tomato Mint Cucumber Salad 40

Day 4: Dinner 42

12-Healthy Green Vegetable Soup 42

Day 5: Breakfast 44

13-Healthy Turmeric Yogurt Bowl 44

Day 5: Lunch 46

14-Anti-Inflammatory Vegetable Soup 46

Day 5: Dinner 48

15-Yummy Turmeric Chicken Vegetable Soup 48

Day 6: Breakfast 50

16-Almond Raisins Cauliflower Rice 50

Day 6: Lunch 52

17-Tofu Turmeric Miso Soup 52

Day 6: Dinner 54

18-Healthy Mixed Roasted Vegetables 54

Day 7: Breakfast 56

19-Creamy Cauliflower Mash 56

Day 7: Lunch 58

20-Delicious Curried Cauliflower Soup 58

Day 7: Dinner 60

21-Squash Cauliflower Curry Soup 60

Day 8: Breakfast 62

22-Tasty Roasted Cauliflower 62

Day 8: Lunch 64

23-Coconut Zucchini Turmeric Soup 64

Day 8: Dinner 66

24-Garlic Mushroom Soup 66

Day 9: Breakfast 68

25-Easy Berry Nut Yogurt 68

Day 9: Lunch 70

26-Tasty and Spicy Lentils 70

Day 9: Dinner 72

27-Delicious Slow-Cooked Coconut Chicken 72

Day 10: Breakfast 74

28-Warm Flaxseed Porridge 74

Day 10: Lunch 76

29-Squash Lentil Stew 76

Day 10: Dinner 78

30-Vegetable Chicken Stir Fry 78

Day 11: Breakfast 80

31-Coconut Ginger Breakfast Muffins 80

Day 11: Lunch 82

32-Easy Roasted Radishes 82

Day 11: Dinner 84

33-Flavorful Salmon with Quinoa 84

Day 12: Breakfast 86

34-Simple Turmeric Lemon Quinoa 86

Day 12: Lunch 88

35-Yummy Tomato Pepper Soup 88

Day 12: Dinner 90

36-Tasty Roasted Cashews Broccoli 90

Day 13: Breakfast 92

37-Tomato Breakfast Omelet 92

Day 13: Lunch 94

38-Spicy Chickpea Kamut Salad 94

Day 13: Dinner 96

39-Healthy Carrot Salad 96

Day 14: Breakfast 98

40-Sweet and Fluffy Coconut Pancakes 98

Day 14: Lunch 100

41-Spicy Cabbage Soup 100

Day 14: Dinner 102

42-Sweet and Sour Green Beans 102

Day 15: Breakfast 104

43-Simple Sweet Potato Fritters 104

Day 15: Lunch 106

44-Lemon Turmeric Lentil Soup 106

Day 15: Dinner 108

45-Creamy Butternut Squash Mash 108

Day 16: Breakfast 110

46-Delicious Breakfast Waffle 110

Day 16: Lunch 112

47-Delicious Baked Broccoli 112

Day 16: Dinner 114

48-Nutritious Salmon Patties 114

Day 17: Breakfast 116

49-Turmeric Oat Flour Pancakes 116

Day 17: Lunch 118

50-Mint Carrot Cucumber Fennel Salad 118

Day 17: Dinner 120

51-Crunchy Coconut Crusted Shrimps 120

Day 18: Breakfast 122

52-Vegetable Breakfast Frittata 122

Day 18: Lunch 124

53-Healthy Lentil Broccoli Stew 124

Day 18: Dinner 126

54-Tasty Tomato Carrot Soup 126

Day 19: Breakfast 128

55-Creamy Scrambled Eggs 128

Day 19: Lunch 130

56-Turmeric Tofu Scrambled 130

Day 19: Dinner 132

57-Creamy Green Asparagus Soup 132

Day 20: Breakfast 134

58-Gingerbread Breakfast Oatmeal 134

Day 20: Lunch 136

59-Chicken Tomato Avocado Salad 136

Day 20: Dinner 138

60-Creamy Coconut Dill Celery Soup 138

Day 21: Breakfast 140

61-Easy Amaranth Breakfast Porridge 140

Day 21: Lunch 142

62-Yummy Mixed Fruit Salad 142

Day 21: Dinner 144

63-Easy Grilled Mushrooms 144

Day 22: Breakfast 146

64-Anti-Inflammatory Pineapple Turmeric Smoothie 146

Day 22: Lunch 148

65-Roasted Carrots 148

Day 22: Dinner 150

66-Parsley Garlic Cauliflower Couscous 150

Day 23: Breakfast 152

67-Quick Quinoa Chia Porridge 152

Day 23: Lunch 154

68-Garlic Mustard Chicken 154

Day 23: Dinner 156

69-Baked Potatoes and Broccoli 156

Day 24: Breakfast 158

70-Yummy Chocolate Cherry Shake 158

Day 24: Lunch 160

71-Creamy Lemon Zucchini Hummus 160

Day 24: Dinner 162

72-Walnuts Apple Chicken Salad 162

Day 25: Breakfast 164

73-Walnut Blueberry Yogurt 164

Day 25: Lunch 166

74-Walnut Beet Orange Salad 166

Day 25: Dinner 168

75-Simple Chicken Patties 168

Day 26: Breakfast 170

76-Blueberry Breakfast Shake 170

Day 26: Lunch 172

77-Simple Marinated Eggplant 172

Day 26: Dinner 174

78-Quick Arugula Almond Peach Salad 174

Day 27: Breakfast 176

79-Mango Turmeric Almond Milk Smoothie 176

Day 27: Lunch 178

80-Sweet Mango Salsa 178

Day 27: Dinner 180

81-Kale Orange Carrot Salad 180

Day 28: Breakfast 182

82-Cauliflower Apple Coconut Porridge 182

Day 28: Lunch 184

83-Spinach Mushroom Egg Scramble 184

Day 28: Dinner 186

84-Artichoke Avocado Spinach Salad 186

Day 29: Breakfast 188

85-Quick Creamy Banana Oatmeal 188

Day 29: Lunch 190

86-Easy Egg Tomato Scramble 190

Day 29: Dinner 192

87-Roasted Rosemary Orange Chicken 192

Day 30: Breakfast 194

88-Cinnamon Carrot Banana Smoothie 194

Day 30: Lunch 196

89-Delicious Tomato Cauliflower Rice 196

Day 30: Dinner 198

90-Baked Mustard Salmon 198

Conversion Chart 200

Key Facts about the Anti-Inflammatory Diet

The "Father of Modern Medicine," Hippocrates of Kos, was firm in his belief that proper nutrition would essentially "keep the doctor away" – as the saying goes. It's not the end of the world if we sometimes make a slight slip from our diets. But going overboard with snacks and other harmful foods is definitely not the healthy choice to make.

When we get an infection, the body's natural reaction is to cause an inflammation in the area to kick the immune system into action. This helps our body mend the wound and regenerate the damaged tissue. Even the definition tells us as much. There is no issue when this type of irritation develops as it is naturally intended.

The only complications arise when the inflammation overstays its welcome. It's simply not healthy for a part of the body to stay irritated for longer than it's supposed to. Not only is it dangerous for the affected area, but also for the rest of your bodily functions. We call this lingering effect chronic inflammation – which can (in some cases) be the underlying cause for more severe conditions, such as Alzheimer's disease, heart problems, and even cancer.

Chronic inflammation can have a variety of causes, but most of them can be counted on one hand:

- First off, living a stressful life;
- Having a genetic susceptibility to the condition;
- Getting little to no exercise;
- Having an unhealthy diet;

As you can see, you're even left with an extra finger after you finish counting them. In any case, this should give you an idea about how to identify the origin of such a dangerous condition, and what you can do to prevent it. In the following paragraphs, we'll be discussing the dietary part on how to minimize the effects of inflammation. Not only will you become healthier as a result, but you don't have to sacrifice taste for some bland recipes. Every one of these recipes is delicious! When you hear the word "diet," the first thing that comes to mind is losing weight. But the anti-inflammatory diet isn't about that. Well, an obvious after-effect of eating healthily as described here is that you will lose weight. We don't think anyone has any complaints about that. Still, this diet's main concern is to give your body the necessary boost to help counteract inflammation over a long period of time. It's a lifestyle change that many people in the modern age could use to become healthier.

Before starting on the anti-inflammatory diet, you should keep some golden rules in mind:

- You need to diversify your menu. For one, you should consider incorporating more fruits and veggies into your meal plan. Five servings should suffice.
- Keep your menu items fresh, and your fruits and vegetables organically grown whenever you can.
- Try not to eat from fast food joints at all, and limit artificial and processed foods in your diet
- Plan your meals in advance, while remembering the first golden rule on this list.

How Will This Diet Help Me?

There are numerous rewards you can reap from undertaking an anti-inflammatory diet, such as:

- A diminished blood pressure;
- Besides safeguarding against chronic inflammation, it can also prevent chronic diseases that arise from it – such as cancer, and others in that category;
- Those suffering from arthritis will be happy to know that the anti-inflammatory diet minimizes its effects;
- Perfect for healthy joints, a healthy heart and cardiovascular system;
- Weight loss is not its main goal, but a definite boon nonetheless, especially for those experiencing joint pain;

How Is Food a Factor in Preventing Inflammation?

Many researchers are discovering that there is a significant daily rise in cancer patients, as well as people suffering a variety of heart conditions. As we have seen so far, chronic inflammation is a great contributor to this sudden increase. It can have a permanent damaging effect on your body's tissues, as well as contribute to an impaired immune system. This depletes your body's natural will to fight against disease, leaving you at risk for cancer and other such serious conditions.

It's not exactly possible to prevent cancer (and others) in 100% of cases just by making dietary changes. If it were, we wouldn't need modern medicine – just a dietician. But it does put up a strong barrier that's hard to break.

All you need to do is understand which foods you should (and shouldn't) eat in order to reduce inflammation. We'll get into that in a moment, and also present some scientific arguments about why it's good (or not) to eat each of these "menu items." Keep on reading!

So Which Foods Are Considered Anti-Inflammatory?

It's a good thing you decided to follow this diet. After all, every climb starts with the first step. It may seem like a daunting task at first because there's a lot of stuff to keep in mind. But just using some of these recipes on a regular basis and you'll be on the right track to getting rid of inflammation one and for all. Give it time, and it'll become second nature to distinguish between harmful and beneficial foods. You won't even need these recipes in front of you to make the correct decisions for a healthier life.

In any case, let's get right down to what foods you should incorporate into your diet:

1) Fish with Plenty of Fatty Acids

Here are some important facts about fish that make them a great addition to an anti-inflammatory diet:

- The omega-3 fatty acids in them are great for their antioxidant properties.
- Any antioxidant minimizes the production of C-reactive protein (CRP) and interleukin-6.
- Those are two proteins that actually cause inflammation.

How much fish should you eat? In one week - anywhere from two to six portions of salmon, mackerel, sardines, etc.

2) Veggies

Vegetables form the basis of any healthy diet, but here's why they're crucial to this one:

- Like fish, many vegetables are high in antioxidant content;
- Not only that, but they're also rich in flavonoids and carotenoids;

How many veggies should you eat? In one day – a minimum of 4 servings (about half a plate) is required to get the full benefits. Stuff like spinach, carrots, peas, and similar items are recommended.

3) Nuts

Just remember not to stuff yourself with salty peanuts – though rich in protein, antioxidants, fibers, and fats (like most nuts), the salt isn't very good for you.

How many nuts should you eat? Incorporate about a handful of almonds, walnuts, and/ or other nuts in your daily menu.

4) Beans and Legumes

Along with the benefits of nuts, this food group also has a high mineral content. They also have a low glycemic index (which means they don't raise your blood sugar levels that much, like other foods). This is perfect for those who think about losing weight with this diet.

How many beans and legumes should you eat? Up to 2 daily portions of things like black beans, peas, etc.

5) Fruit

As with veggies, fruits have a high antioxidant content and are perfect for this diet, provided you get them organically grown.

How much fruit should you eat? About 4 portions daily should suffice, and you can go wild on what choices you have (though apples and various berries are the best.)

6) "Good" Fats

- Good fats (mono-saturated) can be found in seeds of many kinds (like hemp or flax, for example).
- Other than that, you can use about 3 tablespoons of olive oil for cooking or in salads;
- They are crucial for anti-inflammatory meals because of their antioxidant and oleocanthal content (the latter also acts as a natural painkiller).

7) Whole Grains

- These and cracked grains are packed with vital nutrients your body needs;
- Your stomach also processes them at a slower rate than white grains, so they are less inflammatory;

How many whole grains should you eat? Up to 5 portions of things like wild rice, buckwheat, and the like, should be enough.

8) Mushrooms

These are another great food group because they are rich in antioxidants and also have nutrients that improve your immune system. You can basically eat a lot of these (especially shiitake and oyster mushrooms), and combine them with your favorite dishes.

9) Condiments (Herbs)

You can use ginger, garlic, turmeric, and curry powder to spice up any food on your menu – while also benefitting from their powerful anti-inflammatory nature.

As a final note: drink plenty of water (at least 2 liters (9 cups) per day)!

Top 5 Foods that Fight Against Inflammation

While the previous section talked in large lines about anti-inflammatory foods, this one will concentrate on 5 of them we consider the best in the category.

1) Salmon

We've already mentioned the omega-3 fatty acids and high anti-oxidant content in them – but they're a really versatile fish which can be used in a lot of dishes. Of course, there are people who just don't like fish, so try to at least include EPA/DHA fish supplements in your diet.

2) Olive Oil

Extra virgin is recommended. This item can be used in salads (especially) and to cook other dishes (though it should be kept to a minimum). It can protect you from respiratory conditions such as asthma, act as a natural painkiller against arthritis, as well as boosting your cardiovascular system.

3) "Greens"

You know the ones – every kid seems to hate them for some reason (they can be really delicious if cooked right!) Broccoli, kale, spinach, Brussels sprouts, and cauliflower are the "Dangerous 5" when it comes to combating damaging compounds in your body, and their antioxidant properties.

4) Berries

They safeguard your heart from illnesses, as well as keep your brain healthy from mental conditions like dementia. Tart cherries are also great to reduce inflammation, maybe even better than most common over-the-counter painkillers.

5) Turmeric

Spice up your life with this Indian condiment that fights inflammation with a substance called curcumin.

Top 5 Foods You Should Completely Avoid

Not only are these foods not fit for this particular diet, but they're also damaging in every other possible way. No matter how you look at it, these promote obesity, inflammation, and generally make your life worse.

1) Sugar

Public enemy #1 of obesity and heart disease, now you can include inflammation on the long list of reasons you should avoid sugary snacks and juices, though you can consume dark chocolate and dried fruit in moderate amounts.

2) Cooking Oils (that Aren't Olive)

While olive oil is rich in omega-3 fatty acids, these oils (such as sunflower or cottonseed) have omega-6 ones and a generally low content of omega-3's. This disproportion of fatty acids promotes inflammation.

3) Trans Fats

Fast foods are the guilty bunch when it comes to trans fat content, along with processed ones. In essence, anything cooked with margarine and unhealthy cooking oils is to be avoided like wildfire. Unless you want your bad cholesterol levels to increase and be at risk for heart disease, that is.

4) Red Meat

This and processed meats have been shown to activate the body's inflammatory triggers due to the creation of certain antibodies. You can drink some red wine once in a while, though! It promotes healthy blood circulation and is good for the anti-inflammatory diet (in moderate amounts).

5) Refined Grains

These grains have been stripped of all fiber content and your body turns them into sugars quite effortlessly. We've already discussed the harmful effects of that, so no use repeating ourselves.

Day 1: Breakfast

1-Healthy Overnight Oats

Total Time: 15 minutes

Serves: 2

Ingredients:
- 1/2 cup steel cut oats
- 1 1/2 tbsp chia seeds
- 1 tbsp honey
- 1/2 tbsp coconut oil
- 1/4 tsp ginger
- 1/8 tsp black pepper
- 1/4 tsp cardamom
- 1/4 tsp cinnamon
- 1/2 tsp turmeric
- 1 cup coconut milk

Directions:
- In a saucepan, add coconut milk, turmeric, cinnamon, cardamom, pepper, and ginger.

- Stir well and heat over low-medium heat until warm.
- Add coconut oil and honey and stir until honey is dissolved.
- Do not boil the mixture.
- Remove pan from heat and set aside for 10 minutes to cool.
- In a glass jar add chia seeds and oats.
- Now pour coconut milk mixture into the glass jar.
- Close jar with lid tightly and shake the jar until all ingredients well combined.
- Place jar in the refrigerator for overnights.
- Serve with fresh fruits and enjoy.

Nutritional Value (Amount per Serving):

- Calories 536
- Fat 40.6 g
- Carbohydrates 38 g
- Sugar 12.9 g
- Protein 10.3 g
- Cholesterol 0 mg

Day 1: Lunch

2-Warm Turmeric Carrot Soup

Total Time: 20 minutes

Serves: 2

Ingredients:
- 4 carrots, peeled and chopped
- 1/2 tbsp ginger, grated
- 1 tsp turmeric powder
- 3 cups vegetable broth, low sodium
- 2 tsp coconut oil
- 4 garlic cloves, minced
- 1 onion, chopped
- 1 parsnip, peeled and chopped
- 1 tbsp lemon juice
- 1/2 tsp cayenne pepper

Directions:

- Preheat the oven to 350 F.
- In a bowl, add carrots, garlic, onion, parsnip, coconut oil, and cayenne pepper and toss well.
- Spread bowl mixture on baking tray and roast in preheated oven for 15 minutes.
- Once it done then transfer all roasted carrot mixture with ginger, lemon juice, and vegetable broth into the blender and blend until smooth.
- Pour into serving bowl and serve.

Nutritional Value (Amount per Serving):

- Calories 202
- Fat 7.1 g
- Carbohydrates 25.6 g
- Sugar 10.5 g
- Protein 9.8 g
- Cholesterol 0 mg

Day 1: Dinner

3-Yummy Tomato Turmeric Soup

Total Time: 25 minutes

Serves: 2

Ingredients:
- 5 oz cherry tomatoes, halved
- 14 oz tomatoes, diced
- 1 tbsp apple cider vinegar
- 1 tsp basil, dried
- 1 tsp coconut oil
- 2 tsp turmeric powder
- 2 garlic cloves, minced
- 1 small onion, diced
- 1/2 cup vegetable stock, low sodium
- 1/4 tsp pepper
- 1/2 tsp salt

Directions:

- Heat olive oil in a saucepan over medium heat.
- Add garlic and onion in a pan and sauté for a minute.
- Add cherry tomatoes and turmeric and cook until tomatoes soften.
- Add basil, vinegar, apple cider vinegar, vegetable stock and tomatoes. Stir well and bring to boil.
- Cover saucepan with lid and simmer for 5 minutes.
- Using blender puree the soup until smooth.
- Season with pepper and salt.
- Serve warm and enjoy.

Nutritional Value (Amount per Serving):

- Calories 103
- Fat 3.7 g
- Carbohydrates 17.2 g
- Sugar 9 g
- Protein 3 g
- Cholesterol 0 mg

Day 2: Breakfast

4-Delicious Apple Cinnamon Quinoa

Total Time: 25 minutes

Serves: 4

Ingredients:
- 1 cup quinoa, rinsed and drained
- 2 packets stevia
- 1 tsp vanilla extract
- 1 tbsp coconut oil
- 3/4 cup applesauce, unsweetened
- 1 tbsp cinnamon
- 2 cups almond milk, unsweetened
- 1/4 tsp salt

Directions:
- Add quinoa, almond milk, cinnamon and salt in a saucepan and heat over medium-high heat. Bring to boil.

- Reduce heat to low and cover saucepan with lid and cook for 15 minutes.
- Remove pan from heat and set aside for 5 minutes.
- After 5 minutes add sweetener, vanilla extract, coconut oil, and applesauce. Stir well.
- Serve and enjoy.

Nutritional Value (Amount per Serving):

- Calories 489
- Fat 34.6 g
- Carbohydrates 41.6 g
- Sugar 8.8 g
- Protein 8.9 g
- Cholesterol 0 mg

Day 2: Lunch

5-Slow Cooker Broccoli Turmeric Soup

Total Time: 3 hours 10 minutes

Serves: 6

Ingredients:
- 8 cups broccoli florets
- 6 cups vegetable broth, low sodium
- 1 tbsp sesame oil
- 1 tsp ground turmeric
- 2 tbsp ginger, chopped
- 4 cups leeks, chopped
- 2 tbsp olive oil
- 1 tsp salt

Directions:
- Heat olive oil in a pan over medium heat.
- Add chopped leek in a pan and sauté for 8 minutes.

- Add leek, sesame oil, turmeric, broccoli, ginger, broth, and salt in slow cooker and stir well.
- Cover slow cooker with lid and cook on low for 3 hours.
- Using blender puree the soup until smooth and creamy.
- Serve warm and enjoy.

Nutritional Value (Amount per Serving):

- Calories 184
- Fat 9 g
- Carbohydrates 18.9 g
- Sugar 5.1 g
- Protein 9.3 g
- Cholesterol 0 mg

Day 2: Dinner

6-Zucchini Avocado Broccoli Salad

Total Time: 15 minutes

Serves: 2

Ingredients:
- 1 avocado, peeled and diced
- 1 zucchini, sliced
- 1 small broccoli head, cut into florets
- 1/4 cup almonds, toasted and crushed
- 1 tbsp chia seeds
- 1/2 tsp Dijon mustard
- 1 tbsp olive oil
- 1/2 lemon juice
- 1 small onion, sliced
- 1 bunch watercress, rinsed
- 1/2 tsp sea salt

Directions:

- Add all vegetable in a large bowl and toss well.
- In a small bowl, combine together mustard, lemon juice, olive oil, and salt.
- Pour dressing over salad then add almonds and chia seeds. Toss salad well.
- Set salad aside for 5 minutes.
- Serve and enjoy.

Nutritional Value (Amount per Serving):

- Calories 480
- Fat 38.1 g
- Carbohydrates 29.4 g
- Sugar 6 g
- Protein 14.4 g
- Cholesterol 0 mg

Day 3: Breakfast

7-Anti-Inflammatory Chia Turmeric Pudding

Total Time: 10 minutes

Serves: 2

Ingredients:

- 4 tbsp chia seeds
- 1 tbsp honey
- 1/2 tsp cinnamon
- 1/2 tsp turmeric powder
- 2 cups almond milk

Directions:

- Add almond milk, honey, cinnamon, and turmeric powder in a saucepan and stir well.
- Bring almond milk mixture quick boil and simmer for 2 minutes.
- Sieve almond milk mixture into the bowl and add chia seeds. Stir well.
- Pour chia milk mixture into the two jars and place in refrigerator for overnight.
- Top with any fresh fruits and serve chilled.

Nutritional Value (Amount per Serving):

- Calories 899
- Fat 76.5 g
- Carbohydrates 43.8 g
- Sugar 16.7 g
- Protein 18.2 g
- Cholesterol 0 mg

Day 3: Lunch

8-Refrshing Cucumber Salad

Total Time: 15 minutes

Serves: 4

Ingredients:
- 2 lbs cucumbers, sliced
- 1/2 cup fresh dill, chopped
- 1/2 onion, sliced
- For dressing:
- 3 tbsp olive oil
- 4 tbsp white vinegar
- salt

Directions:
- In a bowl, add cucumbers, dill, and onion. Toss well.
- In a small bowl, combine together vinegar and olive oil.
- Pour vinegar mixture over cucumber mixture and toss well.

- Season salad with salt and place in refrigerator.
- Serve chilled and enjoy.

Nutritional Value (Amount per Serving):

- Calories 148
- Fat 11 g
- Carbohydrates 13 g
- Sugar 4.4 g
- Protein 2.8 g
- Cholesterol 0 mg

Day 3: Dinner

9-Tasty Lentil Quinoa Curry

Total Time: 20 minutes

Serves: 4

Ingredients:
- 1 cup lentils, cooked
- 1 cup quinoa, cooked
- 1/4 cup parsley, chopped
- 1 tsp coconut oil
- 1/2 tsp red chili flakes
- 1 tsp curry powder
- 1 tsp turmeric
- 1/2 lemon juice
- 3 tomato, chopped
- 1/2 cup coconut milk
- 3 garlic cloves, minced
- 2 carrots, peeled and diced
- 1 small onion, diced
- 1 tsp sea salt

Directions:

- Heat coconut oil in a saucepan over medium heat.
- Add garlic and onion and cook over low heat for 5 minutes.
- Add chili, turmeric, and curry powder and stir well to combine.
- Add lentils, quinoa, tomatoes and coconut milk. Stir well and bring to boil.
- Reduce heat to low and simmer for 5 minutes.
- Add lemon juice and season with salt.
- Stir well and serve warm.

Nutritional Value (Amount per Serving):

- Calories 442
- Fat 11.7 g
- Carbohydrates 66 g
- Sugar 5.6 g
- Protein 20.3 g
- Cholesterol 0 mg

Day 4: Breakfast

10-Mango Yogurt Overnight Oats

Total Time: 10 minutes

Serves: 2

Ingredients:
- 1/2 cup rolled oats
- 1/2 mango, chopped
- 2 tsp maple syrup
- 1 tbsp chia seeds
- 1/2 cup almond milk
- 1/2 cup plain yogurt
- 1/4 tsp cardamom
- 1/4 tsp cinnamon
- 1/4 tsp ginger
- 1/4 tsp turmeric

Directions:
- Add all ingredients except mango into the glass jar and stir well.
- Place jar in the refrigerator for overnight.

- In the morning pour oat mixture into the two bowls and top with chopped mango.
- Serve and enjoy.

Nutritional Value (Amount per Serving):
- Calories 408
- Fat 21.6 g
- Carbohydrates 44.4 g
- Sugar 22 g
- Protein 11.5 g
- Cholesterol 4 mg

Day 4: Lunch

11-Easy Tomato Mint Cucumber Salad

Total Time: 10 minutes

Serves: 4

Ingredients:
- 3 cucumbers, peeled and diced
- 1 cup fresh mint, chopped
- 1 cup fresh parsley, chopped
- 1/2 onion, chopped
- 2 medium tomatoes, deseed and chopped
- 3 tbsp lemon juice
- 3 tbsp olive oil
- 1/2 tsp pepper
- 1/2 tsp salt

Directions:
- Add cucumbers, mint, parsley, onion and tomatoes in a bowl and toss well.
- In a small bowl, combine together lemon juice and olive oil.

- Pour lemon juice dressing over salad and toss well.
- Season salad with pepper and salt.
- Serve and enjoy.

Nutritional Value (Amount per Serving):

- Calories 159
- Fat 11.3 g
- Carbohydrates 15.1 g
- Sugar 6.3 g
- Protein 3.5 g
- Cholesterol 0 mg

Day 4: Dinner

12-Healthy Green Vegetable Soup

Total Time: 25 minutes

Serves: 2

Ingredients:
- 1 cup fresh spinach
- 1 fennel bulb, diced
- 1/2 cup fresh kale leaves, chopped
- 1 small onion, diced
- 1/4 cup fresh asparagus, chopped
- 2 celery stalks, chopped
- 1 lime juice
- 1 tsp coconut oil
- 2 garlic cloves, minced
- 1 cup vegetable stock, low sodium

Directions:
- Heat coconut oil in a saucepan over medium heat.

- Add garlic, onion, celery, fennel and asparagus in a pan and sauté for 5 minutes over low heat.
- Add vegetable stock in a saucepan and bring to boil.
- Reduce heat to low and simmer for 5 minutes.
- Add spinach and kale. Stir well and remove saucepan from heat.
- Using blender puree the soup until smooth.
- Stir well and serve warm.

Nutritional Value (Amount per Serving):

- Calories 103
- Fat 3.7 g
- Carbohydrates 19.1 g
- Sugar 3.5 g
- Protein 3.5 g
- Cholesterol 0 mg

Day 5: Breakfast

13-Healthy Turmeric Yogurt Bowl

Total Time: 10 minutes

Serves: 2

Ingredients:
- 2 cups plain yogurt
- 1/8 tsp ground cloves
- 1 tsp cinnamon
- 1 tbsp turmeric
- 1 tsp stevia
- 1 tbsp chia seeds
- 1 tsp mint extract
- 1 tsp coconut extract
- For toppings:
- 1 tbsp coconut flakes, unsweetened
- 1/2 cup blueberries
- 1/2 cup raspberries

Directions:

- Add all ingredients except toppings into the bowl and mix well.
- Pour yogurt mixture into the two bowls and top with coconut flakes, blueberries, and raspberries.
- Serve immediately and enjoy.

Nutritional Value (Amount per Serving):

- Calories 319
- Fat 9.4 g
- Carbohydrates 36.3 g
- Sugar 22.8 g
- Protein 18.2 g
- Cholesterol 15 mg

Day 5: Lunch

14-Anti-Inflammatory Vegetable Soup

Total Time: 40 minutes

Serves: 6

Ingredients:
- 1 bunch kale, chopped
- 15 oz can northern beans, rinsed and drained
- 3 cups cauliflower florets, chopped
- 3 cups water
- 32 oz vegetable broth
- 2 stalks celery, chopped
- 1 medium carrot, chopped
- 1 onion, diced
- 1 tbsp olive oil
- 7 oz noodles, drained
- 1/4 tsp cayenne pepper
- 1/2 tsp ground ginger
- 2 tsp garlic, minced

- 1 tbsp ground turmeric
- 1/2 tsp pepper
- 1 tsp salt

Directions:

- In a saucepan, heat olive oil over medium-low heat.
- Add onion in a saucepan and cook for 5 minutes or until onion is lightly brown.
- Add celery and carrots and cook for 3 minutes or until vegetables soften.
- Add cayenne, ginger, garlic, and turmeric and stir for 1 minute.
- Add water, broth, pepper, and salt. Stir well and bring to boil.
- Reduce heat to low and add cauliflower. Stir well and simmer for 10 minutes.
- Once cauliflower is tender then add noodles, kale, and beans and cook until kale is wilted.
- Stir well and serve hot.

Nutritional Value (Amount per Serving):

- Calories 501
- Fat 6.6 g
- Carbohydrates 87.2 g
- Sugar 3.2 g
- Protein 31.5 g
- Cholesterol 10 mg

Day 5: Dinner

15-Yummy Turmeric Chicken Vegetable Soup

Total Time: 30 minutes

Serves: 6

Ingredients:
- 2 large chicken breasts
- 1 1/2 tbsp olive oil
- 1 zucchini, diced
- 2 large potatoes, diced
- 4 parsnips, chopped
- 1 large onion, diced
- 1 cup peas
- 2 tsp cumin
- 1 tbsp turmeric
- 32 oz chicken broth, low sodium
- 6 cups water
- 2 tsp salt

Directions:

- In olive oil in a large saucepan over medium heat.
- Add onion and sauté for 3 minutes.
- Add all remaining vegetables in a pan and sauté for 5 minutes or until softened.
- Add chicken breasts, broth, spices, and water. Stir well.
- Cover saucepan with lid and bring to boil.
- Reduce heat to low and cook until chicken is cooked.
- Remove chicken from saucepan and using fork shred the chicken.
- Return shredded chicken to a pan and simmer for 10 minutes.
- Stir well and serve.

Nutritional Value (Amount per Serving):

- Calories 240
- Fat 5.9 g
- Carbohydrates 31.8 g
- Sugar 6 g
- Protein 15.5 g
- Cholesterol 24 mg

Day 6: Breakfast

16-Almond Raisins Cauliflower Rice

Total Time: 25 minutes

Serves: 2

Ingredients:
- 1 cauliflower head, cut into florets
- 1 tsp black pepper
- 2 tsp turmeric
- 1/2 cup almonds, chopped
- 1/4 cup raisins
- 2 garlic cloves, minced
- 1 large onion, diced
- 1 tbsp olive oil

Directions:
- Add cauliflower florets into the food processor and process until you get rice texture.
- Heat olive oil in a pan over medium heat.
- Add onion to the pan and sauté for 5 minutes.

- Add garlic and stir for 1 minute.
- Add cauliflower rice into the pan and stir-fry for 5 minutes.
- Sprinkle turmeric and black pepper over cauliflower rice and stir for 2 minutes.
- Add chopped almonds and raisins and stir-fry for another 2 minutes.
- Serve hot and enjoy.

Nutritional Value (Amount per Serving):

- Calories 330
- Fat 19.4 g
- Carbohydrates 36.6 g
- Sugar 18.2 g
- Protein 9.5 g
- Cholesterol 0 mg

Day 6: Lunch

17-Tofu Turmeric Miso Soup

Total Time: 25 minutes

Serves: 2

Ingredients:
- 7 oz tofu, cubed
- 1 tbsp white mellow miso
- 1 tsp maple syrup
- 1 tsp apple cider
- 1/2 tsp turmeric
- 3 1/2 cups water
- 1 tsp soy sauce
- 1/2 bell pepper, sliced
- 1/2 carrot, shredded
- 1 tsp ginger, minced
- 7 garlic cloves, chopped
- 1 tsp olive oil
- 1/2 tsp black pepper

- 1/2 tsp salt

Directions:

- Heat olive oil in a saucepan over medium heat.
- Add ginger and garlic and cook for 4 minutes.
- Add peppers and carrots and cook for 3 minutes.
- Add tofu and chopped veggies and stir well.
- Add water and black pepper and remaining ingredients except for miso. Bring to boil.
- Reduce heat and simmer for 4 minutes.
- Add miso and stir well and simmer for few minutes.
- Serve hot and enjoy.

Nutritional Value (Amount per Serving):

- Calories 154
- Fat 6.7 g
- Carbohydrates 15.2 g
- Sugar 5.3 g
- Protein 9.6 g
- Cholesterol 0 mg

Day 6: Dinner

18-Healthy Mixed Roasted Vegetables

Total Time: 40 minutes

Serves: 4

Ingredients:
- 1 lb Brussels sprouts
- 2 sweet potatoes, peeled and diced
- 2 carrots, peeled and sliced
- 4 tbsp coconut oil, melted
- 1 tbsp oregano, dried
- 1 tbsp garlic powder
- 1 tbsp turmeric powder
- 1/4 cup cumin powder
- 1/2 tsp black pepper
- 1/2 tbsp sea salt

Directions:
- Preheat the oven to 350 F.

- Boil Brussels sprouts, sweet potatoes, and carrots for 10 minutes.
- Strain vegetables well and place on baking tray.
- Drizzle vegetables with coconut oil then sprinkle spices over vegetables.
- Roast vegetables in preheated oven for 30 minutes.
- Serve and enjoy.

Nutritional Value (Amount per Serving):

- Calories 275
- Fat 15.7 g
- Carbohydrates 32.7 g
- Sugar 7.4 g
- Protein 6.9 g
- Cholesterol 0 mg

Day 7: Breakfast

19-Creamy Cauliflower Mash

Total Time: 35 minutes

Serves: 2

Ingredients:
- 1 cauliflower head, cut into florets
- 2 sprigs rosemary
- 1 cup water
- 1 tbsp olive oil
- 1/2 tsp garlic, minced
- 1/2 onion, diced

Directions:
- Heat olive oil in frying pan over medium-high heat.
- Add cauliflower, garlic, onion, pepper, and salt in a pan and cook for about 10 minutes or until cauliflower is softened.
- Add water to the pan and simmer over medium heat until all liquid is absorbed.
- Transfer all ingredients to the blender and blend until smooth and creamy.
- Garnish cauliflower mash with rosemary and serve.

Nutritional Value (Amount per Serving):

- Calories 177
- Fat 7.5 g
- Carbohydrates 25.1 g
- Sugar 11.3 g
- Protein 8.7 g
- Cholesterol 0 mg

Day 7: Lunch

20-Delicious Curried Cauliflower Soup

Total Time: 40 minutes

Serves: 10

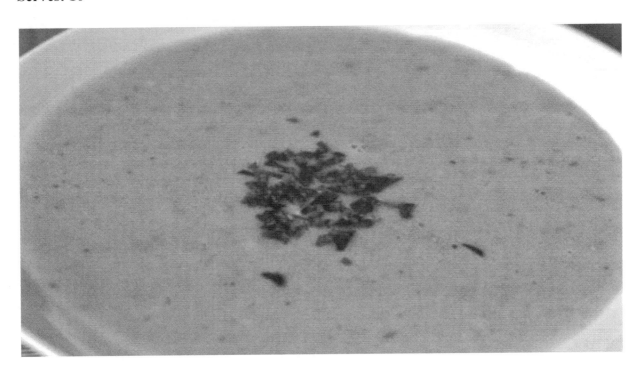

Ingredients:

- 1 medium cauliflower head, cut into florets
- 4 cups vegetable broth, low sodium
- 14 oz can coconut milk
- 1 tsp turmeric
- 2 tbsp curry powder
- 1 tsp ginger, grated
- 2 tsp garlic, minced
- 1 large sweet potato, peeled and diced
- 1 cup onion, diced
- 1 cup carrots, diced
- 1 tbsp coconut oil

Directions:

- Add coconut oil in instant pot and heat oil using sauté function.

- Add onion and carrots and cook for 3 minutes.
- Add cauliflower, sweet potato, turmeric, curry powder, ginger, and garlic. Stir well to combine.
- Add broth and coconut milk and stir well.
- Seal pot with lid and select soup function.
- Release pressure using quick release method than open lid carefully.
- Using blender puree the soup until smooth.
- Season with pepper and salt.
- Serve warm and enjoy.

Nutritional Value (Amount per Serving):

- Calories 151
- Fat 10.7 g
- Carbohydrates 11.6 g
- Sugar 3.9 g
- Protein 4.7 g
- Cholesterol 0 mg

Day 7: Dinner

21-Squash Cauliflower Curry Soup

Total Time: 4 hours 10 minutes

Serves: 4

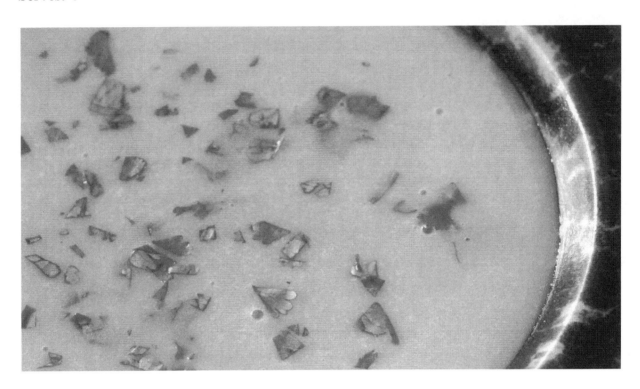

Ingredients:
- 1 small cauliflower head, cut into pieces
- 1 lb butternut squash, peeled and cubed
- 2 tbsp olive oil
- 4 tbsp fresh cilantro, chopped
- 14 oz coconut milk
- 4 cup vegetable broth
- 1 tbsp curry powder
- 1 onion, sliced
- 2 tbsp coconut oil
- 1/4 tsp pepper
- 1 tsp salt

Directions:

- Add all ingredients except cilantro into the slow cooker and mix well.
- Cover slow cooker with lid and cook on high for 4 hours.
- Using blender puree the soup until smooth.
- Garnish with chopped cilantro and serve.

Nutritional Value (Amount per Serving):

- Calories 470
- Fat 39.3 g
- Carbohydrates 26.8 g
- Sugar 9.3 g
- Protein 10.1 g
- Cholesterol 0 mg

Day 8: Breakfast

22-Tasty Roasted Cauliflower

Total Time: 35 minutes

Serves: 4

Ingredients:
- 1 large cauliflower head, cut into florets
- 2 tbsp fresh basil, chopped
- 2 tbsp water
- 1/2 tsp garlic, crushed
- 1/2 tsp red pepper, crushed
- 1/2 tsp cumin
- 1 tsp turmeric
- 2 tbsp coconut oil, melted

Directions:
- Preheat the oven to 400 F.
- In a small bowl, combine together water, garlic, red pepper, cumin, turmeric, and coconut oil.

- In a large bowl, add cauliflower florets then pour small bowl mixture over cauliflower florets and toss well.
- Place cauliflower florets on baking tray and place in preheated oven.
- Roast cauliflower florets in preheated oven for 30 minutes.
- Garnish with chopped basil and serve.

Nutritional Value (Amount per Serving):

- Calories 120
- Fat 7.2 g
- Carbohydrates 12.9 g
- Sugar 5.8 g
- Protein 4.5 g
- Cholesterol 0 mg

Day 8: Lunch

23-Coconut Zucchini Turmeric Soup

Total Time: 20 minutes

Serves: 2

Ingredients:
- 2 medium zucchini, diced
- 1 tbsp coconut oil
- 2 tbsp lime juice
- 1 cup coconut milk
- 1 cup vegetable stock
- 1/4 tsp pepper
- 1 tsp curry powder
- 2 tsp turmeric powder
- 3 garlic cloves, diced
- 1 large onion, diced
- 1/2 tsp salt

Directions:

- Heat coconut oil in a saucepan over medium heat.
- Add onion in a saucepan and sauté for 5 minutes.
- Add garlic, zucchini, and salt in a pan and stir well.
- Add curry powder, turmeric, and pepper and stir for a minute.
- Add coconut milk and stock and stir well. Bring to boil.
- Reduce heat to low and simmer for 10 minutes.
- Add lime juice and stir well.
- Serve hot and enjoy.

Nutritional Value (Amount per Serving):
- Calories 420
- Fat 37.2 g
- Carbohydrates 25 g
- Sugar 11.7 g
- Protein 6.6 g
- Cholesterol 0 mg

Day 8: Dinner

24-Garlic Mushroom Soup

Total Time: 20 minutes

Serves: 4

Ingredients:
- 1 lb mushrooms, sliced
- 2 tbsp tarragon, chopped
- 4 cups vegetable broth
- 1 celery stalk, chopped
- 3 garlic cloves, sliced
- 1 onion, sliced
- 1 tbsp olive oil
- 1/2 tsp pepper
- 1 tsp salt

Directions:
- Heat olive oil in a large saucepan over high heat.
- Add garlic, onion, and celery and sauté for 4 minutes.

- Add mushrooms, pepper, and salt and sauté for 5 minutes.
- Add broth and bring to boil.
- Reduce heat to low and simmer for 5 minutes.
- Stir in tarragon and serve.

Nutritional Value (Amount per Serving):

- Calories 111
- Fat 5.3 g
- Carbohydrates 8.7 g
- Sugar 3.9 g
- Protein 9.1 g
- Cholesterol 0 mg

Day 9: Breakfast

25-Easy Berry Nut Yogurt

Total Time: 10 minutes

Serves: 1

Ingredients:
- 1 cup plain yogurt
- 1 tsp honey
- 1/2 cup berries
- 6 walnuts, chopped

Directions:
- In a bowl, add yogurt and honey and mix well.
- Top yogurt with chopped walnuts and berries.
- Serve immediately and enjoy.

Nutritional Value (Amount per Serving):
- Calories 496
- Fat 29.3 g
- Carbohydrates 36.5 g
- Sugar 29 g

- Protein 20.5 g
- Cholesterol 15 mg

Day 9: Lunch

26-Tasty and Spicy Lentils

Total Time: 30 minutes

Serves: 2

Ingredients:
- 1 cup brown lentils, soaked overnight
- 1 tbsp olive oil
- 1 tsp cumin
- 1 tsp ground chili
- 1 garlic clove, sliced
- 1 tsp majoram
- 1 tsp turmeric
- 1/2 tsp salt

Directions:
- In a saucepan, add lentils, 2 cups water, and salt and cook over medium heat. Bring to boil.
- Reduce heat to low and simmer for 10 minutes.

- Add majoram, chili, turmeric, and garlic and stir well.
- Remove saucepan from heat and add olive oil.
- Stir well and serve.

Nutritional Value (Amount per Serving):

- Calories 409
- Fat 8.4 g
- Carbohydrates 59.4 g
- Sugar 2 g
- Protein 25.2 g
- Cholesterol 0 mg

Day 9: Dinner

27-Delicious Slow-Cooked Coconut Chicken

Total Time: 6 hours 10 minutes

Serves: 6

Ingredients:
- 6 chicken thighs
- 2 scallions, sliced
- 4 tbsp fresh cilantro, chopped
- 3 cups chicken broth, low sodium
- 14 oz coconut milk
- 2 tsp curry powder
- 2 garlic cloves, minced
- 1 onion, sliced
- 1 tbsp coconut oil, melted
- 1/4 tsp pepper
- 1 tsp salt

Directions:

- Add coconut oil into the slow cooker.
- Add all ingredients except scallions and cilantro into the slow cooker and stir well.
- Cover slow cooker with lid and cook on high for 6 hours.
- Serve hot and enjoy.

Nutritional Value (Amount per Serving):

- Calories 334
- Fat 25.9 g
- Carbohydrates 7 g
- Sugar 3.5 g
- Protein 23.4 g
- Cholesterol 0 mg

Day 10: Breakfast

28-Warm Flaxseed Porridge

Total Time: 10 minutes

Serves: 1

Ingredients:
- 1/4 cup ground flaxseeds
- 1/4 tsp cinnamon
- 1 medium banana, mashed
- 1 cup almond milk
- 1 tbsp walnuts, chopped
- 1/8 cup blueberries

Directions:
- Add flaxseeds, cinnamon, banana, and almond milk in saucepan and heat over medium heat.
- Stir well and cook porridge until thicken about 5 minutes.
- Remove porridge from heat and pour in serving bowl.
- Top with chopped walnuts and blueberries.

- Serve warm and enjoy.

Nutritional Value (Amount per Serving):
- Calories 865
- Fat 71.1 g
- Carbohydrates 52.1 g
- Sugar 24.8 g
- Protein 14 g
- Cholesterol 0 mg

Day 10: Lunch

29-Squash Lentil Stew

Total Time: 30 minutes

Serves: 4

Ingredients:
- 1 cup red lentils
- 3 cups butternut squash, cooked
- 1 cup spinach, chopped
- 4 cups vegetable broth, low sodium
- 1 tbsp curry powder
- 3 garlic cloves, minced
- 1 onion, chopped
- 1 tsp olive oil
- 1/2 tsp pepper
- 1/2 tsp salt

Directions:
- In a saucepan, heat olive oil over medium-low heat.

- Add onion and garlic in a saucepan and sauté for 5 minutes.
- Add curry powder in a pan sauté for a minute.
- Add lentils and broth and bring to boil.
- Reduce heat to low and simmer for 10 minutes.
- Stir in spinach and cooked butternut squash and cook for 5 minutes.
- Season with pepper and salt.
- Serve warm and enjoy.

Nutritional Value (Amount per Serving):

- Calories 287
- Fat 3.5 g
- Carbohydrates 46.7 g
- Sugar 5.2 g
- Protein 19.2 g
- Cholesterol 0 mg

Day 10: Dinner

30-Vegetable Chicken Stir Fry

Total Time: 30 minutes

Serves: 6

Ingredients:
- 1 lb chicken thighs, skinless and boneless, cut into strips
- 1 tbsp sesame seeds
- 1 tsp coconut amino
- 1 tsp sesame oil
- 1/2 cup chicken broth
- 1/4 tsp red pepper flakes
- 1 tsp fresh ginger, minced
- 2 carrots, cut into strips
- 2 cups broccoli florets
- 1 tbsp coconut oil
- 1 garlic clove, minced
- 1 tsp salt

Directions:
- In a large pan, heat coconut oil over high heat.

- Add chicken to the pan and sauté for 8 minutes or until chicken brown.
- Stir in carrots, ginger, garlic, broccoli, broth, red pepper flakes, and salt.
- Cover pan with lid and cook for 5 minutes.
- Remove pan from heat and stir in sesame seeds, coconut amino, and sesame oil.
- Stir well and serve hot.

Nutritional Value (Amount per Serving):
- Calories 202
- Fat 9.6 g
- Carbohydrates 5 g
- Sugar 1.6 g
- Protein 23.6 g
- Cholesterol 67 mg

Day 11: Breakfast

31-Coconut Ginger Breakfast Muffins

Total Time: 30 minutes

Serves: 8

Ingredients:
- 6 large organic eggs
- 1/2 tsp ginger powder
- 2 tsp turmeric
- 1/2 tsp baking soda
- 3/4 cup coconut flour
- 2 tbsp coconut flour
- 1 tsp vanilla extract
- 1/3 cup maple syrup
- 1/2 cup coconut milk, unsweetened
- Pepper
- Salt

Directions:

- Preheat the oven to 350 F.
- Spray muffin tray with cooking spray and set aside.
- In a large bowl, add eggs, vanilla, maple syrup, and almond milk and whisk until well combined.
- In another bowl, sift together coconut flour, ginger powder, turmeric, baking soda, pepper, and salt.
- Slowly add dry ingredients into the wet ingredients and mix until well combined.
- Pour batter into the prepared muffin tray and bake in preheated oven for 25 minutes.
- Serve and enjoy.

Nutritional Value (Amount per Serving):

- Calories 147
- Fat 8.1 g
- Carbohydrates 13.2 g
- Sugar 9 g
- Protein 5.8 g
- Cholesterol 140 mg

Day 11: Lunch

32-Easy Roasted Radishes

Total Time: 40 minutes

Serves: 3

Ingredients:
- 21 oz bunches radishes, washed, cleaned and diced
- 2 tsp fresh rosemary, chopped
- 2 tsp fresh lemon juice
- 1 tbsp coconut oil, melted
- Pepper
- Salt

Directions:
- Preheat the oven to 350 F.
- Spray a baking tray with cooking spray and set aside.
- In a bowl, add radishes, pepper, coconut oil, and salt. Mix well.
- Place radishes mixture on a prepared baking tray and roast in preheated oven for 35 minutes. Stir once.

- When done toss with rosemary and lemon juice.
- Serve and enjoy.

Nutritional Value (Amount per Serving):

- Calories 74
- Fat 4.9 g
- Carbohydrates 7.4 g
- Sugar 3.8 g
- Protein 1.4 g
- Cholesterol 0 mg

Day 11: Dinner

33-Flavorful Salmon with Quinoa

Total Time: 30 minutes

Serves: 4

Ingredients:
- 1 lb salmon fillets
- 2 cups quinoa, cooked
- 1 tbsp apple cider vinegar
- 4 tbsp olives, chopped
- 1/2 cup fresh basil, chopped
- 2 cups cherry tomatoes, halved
- 1 onion, diced
- 1 tbsp olive oil
- Pepper
- Salt

Directions:
- Preheat the oven to 375 F.

- Spray a baking tray with cooking spray and set aside.
- Place salmon fillets on prepared baking tray and season with pepper and salt.
- Place the baking tray in preheated oven and bake for 20 minutes.
- Heat olive oil in a large pan over medium-high heat.
- Add onion in a pan and sauté for 3 minutes.
- Stir in quinoa, vinegar, olives, basil and cherry tomatoes. Cook for 2 minutes.
- Place to quinoa mixture on serving dish then place baked salmon over quinoa mixture.
- Serve warm and enjoy.

Nutritional Value (Amount per Serving):

- Calories 531
- Fat 16.8 g
- Carbohydrates 61.3 g
- Sugar 3.6 g
- Protein 35.3 g
- Cholesterol 50 mg

Day 12: Breakfast

34-Simple Turmeric Lemon Quinoa

Total Time: 25 minutes

Serves: 4

Ingredients:
- 1 cup quinoa, rinsed and drained
- 1 1/2 tsp turmeric powder
- 1 tbsp fresh lemon juice
- 1 tsp coconut oil
- 1/2 tsp salt

Directions:
- Cook quinoa until fluffy about 15 minutes.
- Allow to quinoa slightly cool. When it's warm then add all remaining ingredients and stir well.
- Serve immediately and enjoy.

Nutritional Value (Amount per Serving):

- Calories 170
- Fat 3.8 g
- Carbohydrates 27.9 g
- Sugar 0.1 g
- Protein 6.1 g
- Cholesterol 0 mg

Day 12: Lunch

35-Yummy Tomato Pepper Soup

Total Time: 3 hours 15 minutes

Serves: 4

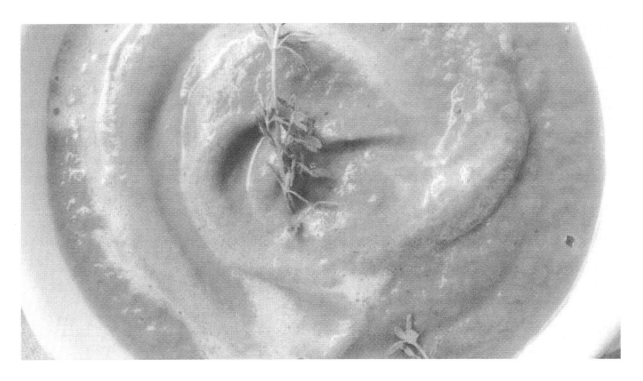

Ingredients:
- 28 oz tomatoes, chopped
- 12 oz red peppers, roasted
- 3 cups vegetable broth
- 1/2 tsp pepper
- 1/2 tsp thyme, dried
- 1/2 tsp basil, dried
- 1 tbsp turmeric
- 1 tbsp coconut oil
- 4 garlic cloves, minced
- 1 onion, diced

Directions:
- Heat coconut oil in large pan over medium heat.
- Add onion and garlic in a pan and sauté for 2 minutes.

- Add turmeric, thyme, basil, and pepper and stir for 30 seconds.
- Add pan mixture into the slow cooker then add tomatoes, peppers, and vegetable broth. Stir well.
- Cover slow cooker with lid and cook on low for 3 hours.
- Using blender puree the soup until smooth.
- Stir well and serve.

Nutritional Value (Amount per Serving):

- Calories 150
- Fat 5.4 g
- Carbohydrates 20.8 g
- Sugar 11.5 g
- Protein 7.6 g
- Cholesterol 0 mg

Day 12: Dinner

36-Tasty Roasted Cashews Broccoli

Total Time: 30 minutes

Serves: 4

Ingredients:
- 6 cups broccoli florets
- 1/2 cup cashews, roasted
- 1 tbsp coconut amino
- 2 tbsp olive oil
- 1 tsp salt

Directions:
- Preheat the oven to 375 F.
- In a bowl, add broccoli, salt, and olive oil. Toss well.
- Place broccoli on a baking tray and bake in preheated oven for 15 minutes.
- In a large mixing bowl, add roasted broccoli, cashews and coconut amino and toss well.
- Serve and enjoy.

Nutritional Value (Amount per Serving):
- Calories 209

- Fat 15.4 g
- Carbohydrates 15.4 g
- Sugar 3.2 g
- Protein 6.4 g
- Cholesterol 0 mg

Day 13: Breakfast

37-Tomato Breakfast Omelet

Total Time: 15 minutes

Serves: 2

Ingredients:
- 4 large organic eggs
- 1/4 cup tomato, diced
- 2 green onion, chopped
- 1/8 tsp turmeric
- 1/4 tsp mustard seeds
- 1 tbsp olive oil
- 3/8 tsp kosher salt
- Pepper

Directions:
- In a bowl, whisk together egg and salt.
- Heat olive oil in a pan over medium-high heat.
- Add turmeric and mustard in a pan and cook for 30 seconds.
- Add onion and cook until softened.

- Add diced tomato and cook for 1 minute.
- Now add egg mixture into the pan and cook until edges are set about 2 minutes.
- Flip omelet to other side and cook for another 2 minutes.
- Fold omelet in half and transfer to serving the dish.
- Serve and enjoy.

Nutritional Value (Amount per Serving):

- Calories 214
- Fat 17.2 g
- Carbohydrates 3 g
- Sugar 1.7 g
- Protein 13.2 g
- Cholesterol 372 mg

Day 13: Lunch

38-Spicy Chickpea Kamut Salad

Total Time: 10 minutes

Serves: 4

Ingredients:
- 1 cup chickpeas, soaked overnight and boiled
- 1 cup Kamut, cooked
- 1/2 tbsp lemon juice
- 1 tbsp balsamic vinegar
- 1/2 tsp turmeric
- 1/2 tsp thyme
- 1 tsp paprika
- 1 tbsp olive oil
- 1 garlic clove, minced
- 6 grape tomatoes, chopped
- Pepper
- Salt

Directions:

- Add tomato, chickpeas, and Kamut in a bowl and mix well.
- In a small bowl, combine together turmeric, thyme, paprika, oil, and garlic. Add in chickpea mixture and mix well.
- Pour vinegar and lemon juice over salad and toss well.
- Season salad with pepper and salt.
- Serve and enjoy.

Nutritional Value (Amount per Serving):

- Calories 327
- Fat 7 g
- Carbohydrates 54.4 g
- Sugar 10.3 g
- Protein 14.5 g
- Cholesterol 0 mg

Day 13: Dinner

39-Healthy Carrot Salad

Total Time: 15 minutes

Serves: 2

Ingredients:
- 3 carrots, peeled and cut into strips
- 1 tsp lime zest
- 1 tbsp lemon juice
- 4 tbsp raisins
- 1/3 tsp cinnamon
- 1/3 cup olives
- 3 tbsp plain yogurt
- 1 tsp salt

Directions:
- Add carrots, lime zest, raisins, olive, and salt in a bowl and toss well.
- In a small bowl, combine together lemon juice, cinnamon, and yogurt.
- Pour dressing over salad and serve.

Nutritional Value (Amount per Serving):

- Calories 137
- Fat 2.8 g
- Carbohydrates 27 g
- Sugar 17.1 g
- Protein 2.9 g
- Cholesterol 1 mg

Day 14: Breakfast

40-Sweet and Fluffy Coconut Pancakes

Total Time: 25 minutes

Serves: 8

Ingredients:
- 3 organic eggs
- 1/2 tsp vanilla extract
- 1 tbsp honey
- 2 tbsp coconut oil
- 1/4 cup coconut milk
- 1/8 tsp baking soda
- 1/4 cup coconut flour
- Pinch of salt

Directions:
- In a bowl, whisk together eggs, honey, and coconut oil.
- Add vanilla extract and coconut milk and stir well.
- Add coconut flour, salt, and baking soda and mix well to combine.
- Heat pan over medium heat and add spread butter on the pan.

- Now add batter and make pancakes and cook until lightly golden brown from both the sides.
- Serve immediately and enjoy.

Nutritional Value (Amount per Serving):
- Calories 81
- Fat 6.9 g
- Carbohydrates 3 g
- Sugar 2.6 g
- Protein 2.3 g
- Cholesterol 61 mg

Day 14: Lunch

41-Spicy Cabbage Soup

Total Time: 35 minutes

Serves: 4

Ingredients:
- 1 cabbage head, chopped
- 2 tbsp coconut oil
- 3 cups vegetable stock
- 1/4 cup coconut milk
- 1 tsp ground cumin
- 2 tsp ground turmeric
- 2 garlic cloves, chopped
- 1/2 tsp pepper
- 1/2 tsp salt

Directions:
- Heat coconut oil in a saucepan over medium heat.
- Add cabbage and garlic in a pan and sauté for 10 minutes or until cabbage is softened.
- Add vegetable stock and stir well.

- Cover saucepan and simmer for 20 minutes.
- Remove saucepan from heat and add coconut milk and spices.
- Using blender puree the soup until smooth.
- Season with pepper and salt.
- Serve warm and enjoy.

Nutritional Value (Amount per Serving):

- Calories 149
- Fat 11.3 g
- Carbohydrates 13.3 g
- Sugar 6.8 g
- Protein 2.9 g
- Cholesterol 0 mg

Day 14: Dinner

42-Sweet and Sour Green Beans

Total Time: 20 minutes

Serves: 6

Ingredients:
- 1 lb green beans
- 1 tbsp garlic, minced
- 1 tbsp olive oil
- 2 tbsp almond flakes
- 1 cup chicken stock
- 1 tbsp water
- 1 tbsp apple cider vinegar
- 1 tsp salt

Directions:
- Add chicken stock in a large saucepan and bring to boil.
- Add green beans and salt in a pan.
- Cover pan with lid and simmer for 15 minutes.

- Remove chicken stock from saucepan.
- In a small bowl combine together almond flakes, water, vinegar, olive oil, and garlic.
- Pour almond flakes mixture over green beans.
- Cover pan with lid and cook for 5 minutes.
- Serve hot and enjoy.

Nutritional Value (Amount per Serving):

- Calories 75
- Fat 4.9 g
- Carbohydrates 6.3 g
- Sugar 1.4 g
- Protein 2.7 g
- Cholesterol 0 mg

Day 15: Breakfast

43-Simple Sweet Potato Fritters

Total Time: 15 minutes

Serves: 8

Ingredients:
- 2 1/2 cups sweet potato, shredded
- 1 large organic egg, beaten
- 1/2 cup scallions, chopped
- 1/3 cup quinoa flour
- 2 tbsp coconut oil
- salt

Directions:
- Add all ingredients except coconut oil in a bowl and mix well until combined.
- Heat coconut oil in a pan over medium heat.
- Once the oil is hot then make small patties from mixture and place on hot pan.
- Cook fritters for 2 minutes on each side or until lightly golden brown.
- Serve warm and enjoy.

Nutritional Value (Amount per Serving):

- Calories 115
- Fat 4.6 g
- Carbohydrates 14.6 g
- Sugar 4.3 g
- Protein 3.8 g
- Cholesterol 23 mg

Day 15: Lunch

44-Lemon Turmeric Lentil Soup

Total Time: 1 hour 35 minutes

Serves: 8

Ingredients:
- 2 cups green lentils, rinsed and drained
- 3 lemon juice
- 1/2 lemon zest
- 2 tsp turmeric
- 32 oz vegetable broth
- 4 tsp ginger, grated
- 3 garlic cloves, minced
- 1 tsp salt
- 1 1/2 cups celery, diced
- 1 1/2 cups carrots, diced
- 1 onion, diced
- 1 tbsp olive oil

Directions:

- Heat olive oil in a large saucepan over medium heat.
- Add onion, celery, carrots, and salt in a pan and sauté for 5 minutes.
- Add ginger and garlic and sauté for a minute.
- Add lentils, turmeric, and broth and stir well.
- Reduce heat to low and cover saucepan with lid and simmer for 45 minutes.
- Stir in lemon juice and zest. Cover and simmer for another 30 minutes.
- Stir well and serve.

Nutritional Value (Amount per Serving):

- Calories 228
- Fat 3.1 g
- Carbohydrates 35 g
- Sugar 3.3 g
- Protein 15.3 g
- Cholesterol 0 mg

Day 15: Dinner

45-Creamy Butternut Squash Mash

Total Time: 40 minutes

Serves: 8

Ingredients:

- 3 lbs butternut squash, chopped
- 1/4 cup almond milk
- 1 tsp oregano
- 1 garlic cloves, sliced
- 2 tbsp olive oil
- 1 tsp cinnamon

Directions:

- Preheat the oven to 365 F.
- In a bowl, add butternut squash, oregano, olive oil and garlic and toss well.
- Place squash mixture on a baking tray and bake in preheated oven for 30 minutes.
- Combine together almond milk and cinnamon and set aside.
- Once squash is baked then allow to cool for 5 minutes.

- Add butternut squash in a blender and blend until smooth.
- Add almond milk mixture and blend until combined.
- Pour into the bowl and serve.

Nutritional Value (Amount per Serving):

- Calories 126
- Fat 5.5 g
- Carbohydrates 20.8 g
- Sugar 4 g
- Protein 1.9 g
- Cholesterol 0 mg

Day 16: Breakfast

46-Delicious Breakfast Waffle

Total Time: 20 minutes

Serves: 2

Ingredients:
- 2 large organic eggs
- 1 cup almond flour
- 2 tsp stevia
- 1/4 cup applesauce, unsweetened
- 1/2 tsp vanilla extract
- 1 tbsp coconut oil
- 1/2 tsp baking powder
- Pinch of salt

Directions:
- Preheat the waffle iron.
- Add all ingredients into the mixing bowl and mix well until combined.
- Spray waffle iron with cooking spray.

- Pour batter into the hot waffle iron and cook according to waffle iron directions.
- Top with fresh berries and serve.

Nutritional Value (Amount per Serving):

- Calories 227
- Fat 18.8 g
- Carbohydrates 9.6 g
- Sugar 4.1 g
- Protein 9.3 g
- Cholesterol 186 mg

Day 16: Lunch

47-Delicious Baked Broccoli

Total Time: 25 minutes

Serves: 6

Ingredients:
- 2 lbs broccoli, cut into florets
- 1/2 tsp turmeric
- 1 tsp parsley
- 1 tsp dill
- 1 tbsp olive oil
- 4 oz almond flakes
- 1 tsp salt
- 1 tbsp sesame oil
- 1 tsp ground ginger
- 2 tbsp garlic, minced

Directions:
- Preheat the oven to 365 F.

- Add all ingredients into the large bowl and toss well.
- Place broccoli mixture on a baking tray and bake in preheated oven for 20 minutes.
- Once done then allow to cool for 5 minutes.
- Serve immediately and enjoy.

Nutritional Value (Amount per Serving):

- Calories 220
- Fat 15.7 g
- Carbohydrates 12.6 g
- Sugar 3.4 g
- Protein 9.3 g
- Cholesterol 0 mg

Day 16: Dinner

48-Nutritious Salmon Patties

Total Time: 20 minutes

Serves: 9

Ingredients:
- 2 lbs salmon fillet, minced
- 1 tsp turmeric
- 1 tbsp olive oil
- 1 tsp salt
- 1 tbsp coconut flour
- 1 zucchini, grated
- 1 tbsp onion powder
- 4 garlic cloves, minced
- 1 tsp parsley, chopped
- 1/2 cup dill, chopped
- 1 onion, chopped

Directions:

- Add all ingredients except olive oil in a mixing bowl and mix well to combine.
- Heat a large pan over medium heat.
- Pour olive oil over the hot pan.
- Make small patties from salmon mixture and place on hot pan.
- Cook patties for 2 minutes on each side or until cooked.
- Serve hot and enjoy.

Nutritional Value (Amount per Serving):

- Calories 174
- Fat 8.2 g
- Carbohydrates 5.5 g
- Sugar 1.3 g
- Protein 20.9 g
- Cholesterol 44 mg

Day 17: Breakfast

49-Turmeric Oat Flour Pancakes

Total Time: 20 minutes

Serves: 5

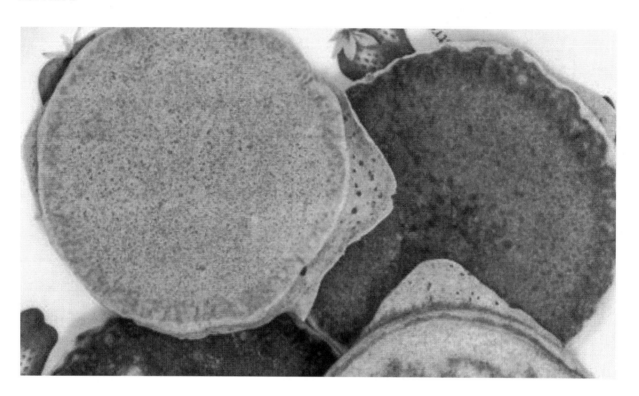

Ingredients:
- 1 1/4 cups oat flour
- 1/4 tsp ginger
- 1/2 tsp ground turmeric
- 1/2 tsp cinnamon
- 1 tsp vanilla extract
- 1 tbsp baking powder
- 2 tbsp maple syrup
- 1/2 cup almond milk
- 1/2 cup applesauce, unsweetened

Directions:
- Add all ingredients into the blender and blend until combined.
- Heat non-stick pan over medium-high heat.

- Pour 1/4 cup batter into hot pan and spread evenly.
- Cook pancake for 2 minutes on each side.
- Serve and enjoy.

Nutritional Value (Amount per Serving):

- Calories 184
- Fat 7.3 g
- Carbohydrates 27.1 g
- Sugar 8.1 g
- Protein 3.6 g
- Cholesterol 0 mg

Day 17: Lunch

50-Mint Carrot Cucumber Fennel Salad

Total Time: 15 minutes

Serves: 4

Ingredients:
- 6 carrots, sliced
- 1 cup fresh parsley, chopped
- 1 fennel bulb, sliced
- 1 cucumber, sliced
- 1/2 cup fresh mint, chopped
- 4 tbsp lemon juice
- 2 tbsp olive oil
- Pepper
- Salt

Directions:
- Add mint, parsley, carrots, fennel, and cucumber in a large bowl and mix well.
- In a small bowl, combine together olive oil and lemon juice.

- Pour dressing over salad and toss well.
- Serve immediately and enjoy.

Nutritional Value (Amount per Serving):

- Calories 141
- Fat 7.5 g
- Carbohydrates 18.2 g
- Sugar 6.2 g
- Protein 2.9 g
- Cholesterol 0 mg

Day 17: Dinner

51-Crunchy Coconut Crusted Shrimps

Total Time: 25 minutes

Serves: 4

Ingredients:
- 15 oz shrimp, peeled
- 1 tsp olive oil
- 1 tsp lemon juice
- 1 tsp turmeric
- 1/2 cup almond milk
- 1/2 cup coconut, shredded
- 1 tsp black pepper

Directions:
- Preheat the oven to 360 F.
- In a bowl, add shrimp, pepper, lemon juice and turmeric. Toss well and set aside for 5 minutes.
- Sprinkle shrimp with olive oil.
- Dip shrimp in almond milk and then coat with coconut.

- Place shrimp on a baking tray and bake in preheated oven for 10 minutes.
- Serve warm and enjoy.

Nutritional Value (Amount per Serving):

- Calories 244
- Fat 13.5 g
- Carbohydrates 5.5 g
- Sugar 1.7 g
- Protein 25.4 g
- Cholesterol 224 mg

Day 18: Breakfast

52-Vegetable Breakfast Frittata

Total Time: 25 minutes

Serves: 2

Ingredients:
- 3 large organic eggs
- 1 tbsp olive oil
- 2 tbsp almond milk
- 1/2 bell pepper, chopped
- 1 tbsp chives, chopped
- 1 garlic clove, minced
- 1/2 onion, chopped
- 1 cup spinach, chopped
- 1 1/2 cups asparagus spears, cut into 1-inch pieces
- Pepper
- Salt

Directions:
- In a bowl, beat eggs and milk and set aside.

- In boiling water blanch asparagus.
- Preheat the oven to 375 F.
- Heat olive oil in an oven-safe skillet.
- Add garlic and onion to skillet and sauté until onion soften.
- Add spinach and bell pepper and sauté until spinach water is evaporated.
- Add chives and asparagus and stir well.
- Spread evenly veggie mixture on the bottom of skillet then pour egg mixture over vegetables.
- Season with pepper and salt.
- Place skillet in preheated oven and bake for 15 minutes or until top is lightly golden brown.
- Cut into pieces and serve.

Nutritional Value (Amount per Serving):

- Calories 249
- Fat 18.4 g
- Carbohydrates 11.3 g
- Sugar 5.8 g
- Protein 13.2 g
- Cholesterol 279 mg

Day 18: Lunch

53-Healthy Lentil Broccoli Stew

Total Time: 30 minutes

Serves: 4

Ingredients:
- 6 cups broccoli florets
- 1/4 cup parsley, chopped
- 1/2 cup green olives, pitted and sliced
- 1 tsp oregano, dried
- 1 cup brown lentils, dried
- 2 cups vegetable broth
- 2 garlic cloves, minced
- 1 carrots, chopped
- 1 onion, chopped
- 1 tbsp olive oil
- 1 tsp salt

Directions:
- Heat olive oil in large pot over high heat.

- Add garlic, onion, and carrots and sauté for 5 minutes.
- Add broth, oregano, and lentils and bring to boil.
- Reduce heat to low and cook for 15 minutes or until lentils tender.
- Add broccoli florets to the pot and simmer for 5 minutes.
- Remove pot from heat and stir in parsley and olives.
- Stir well and serve.

Nutritional Value (Amount per Serving):

- Calories 306
- Fat 7 g
- Carbohydrates 44.5 g
- Sugar 5.6 g
- Protein 19.4 g
- Cholesterol 0 mg

Day 18: Dinner

54-Tasty Tomato Carrot Soup

Total Time: 1 hour 20 minutes

Serves: 6

Ingredients:
- 1 carrot, peeled and cut into small pieces
- 2 tomatoes, chopped
- 1 tbsp ginger, grated
- 1 onion, chopped
- 1 tsp pepper
- 1 tsp cumin
- 5 cups vegetable broth, low sodium
- 4 tbsp olive oil
- 1 cup coriander, chopped
- 2 garlic clove, minced
- 2 tsp salt

Directions:
- Heat olive oil in a saucepan over medium heat.
- Add onion, ginger, garlic and carrots in pan and sauté for 5 minutes over medium heat.

- Add tomatoes and chopped coriander sauté for another 5 minutes.
- Add remaining ingredients and bring to boil.
- Cover pan with lid and simmer over medium-low heat for 60 minutes.
- Using blender puree the soup until smooth.
- Stir well and serve hot.

Nutritional Value (Amount per Serving):
- Calories 138
- Fat 10 g
- Carbohydrates 6 g
- Sugar 3 g
- Protein 5 g
- Cholesterol 0 mg

Day 19: Breakfast

55-Creamy Scrambled Eggs

Total Time: 20 minutes

Serves: 2

Ingredients:
- 4 organic eggs
- 1 tbsp coconut oil
- 1/4 cup almond milk
- 1/2 onion, diced
- 6 sage leaves, chopped
- Pepper
- Salt

Directions:
- Heat coconut oil in large pan over medium heat.
- Add onion to the pan and sauté for 5 minutes.
- In a bowl, whisk together egg and almond milk.
- Once onion softens then add egg mixture, sage, and salt in a pan.

- Cook eggs on low heat. Gently stir eggs and cook for about 5 minutes.
- Season with black pepper and serve.

Nutritional Value (Amount per Serving):

- Calories 268
- Fat 22.9 g
- Carbohydrates 5.6 g
- Sugar 2.9 g
- Protein 12.2 g
- Cholesterol 327 mg

Day 19: Lunch

56-Turmeric Tofu Scrambled

Total Time: 15 minutes

Serves: 2

Ingredients:
- 14 oz tofu
- 1/4 tsp turmeric powder
- 1/4 bell pepper, chopped
- 2 tsp olive oil
- 2 tbsp seasoning
- 1/2 cup onion, chopped
- 1 garlic clove, minced
- Salt

Directions:
- Heat 1 teaspoon olive oil in a pan over medium heat and add chopped onion, garlic and bell pepper sauté for 3 minutes.
- Remove pan from heat and set aside.

- In a bowl, crumbled tofu and mix with seasoning.
- In another pan heat remaining oil. Add turmeric powder and stir well.
- Add crumbled tofu in the pan and stir for 3 minutes.
- Add onion and pepper mixture in tofu and stir well.
- Serve hot and enjoy.

Nutritional Value (Amount per Serving):

- Calories 198
- Fat 13.1 g
- Carbohydrates 7.9 g
- Sugar 3.2 g
- Protein 16.8 g
- Cholesterol 0 mg

Day 19: Dinner

57-Creamy Green Asparagus Soup

Total Time: 35 minutes

Serves: 4

Ingredients:
- 1 lb asparagus, sliced
- 2 garlic cloves, crushed
- 3/4 tsp fresh thyme, chopped
- 1/2 tbsp fresh lemon juice
- 1 bay leaf
- 1/4 tsp lemon zest, grated
- 2 cups coconut milk
- 2 cups vegetable broth
- 1 tsp salt
- Pepper

Directions:
- In a saucepan add asparagus, garlic, bay leaf, thyme, coconut milk and vegetable broth.

- Bring to boil over medium-high heat for 10 minutes.
- Discard bay leaf from the saucepan and using blender puree the soup until smooth.
- Remove from heat and strain.
- Stir in lemon juice, lemon zest, salt and pepper.
- Serve hot and enjoy.

Nutritional Value (Amount per Serving):

- Calories 321
- Fat 29 g
- Carbohydrates 12 g
- Sugar 6 g
- Protein 7 g
- Cholesterol 0 mg

Day 20: Breakfast

58-Gingerbread Breakfast Oatmeal

Total Time: 15 minutes

Serves: 4

Ingredients:
- 1 cup steel cut oats
- 1/4 tsp ground cardamom
- 1/8 tsp ground nutmeg
- 1/4 tsp ground allspice
- 1/4 tsp ground ginger
- 1 tsp ground cloves
- 1/4 tsp ground coriander
- 1 1/2 tbsp ground cinnamon
- 1 cup steel cut oats
- 4 cups water

Directions:
- Add oats with remaining all ingredients into the saucepan and stir well.

- Cook oats mixture according to the packet instructions.
- Serve and enjoy.

Nutritional Value (Amount per Serving):
- Calories 257
- Fat 4.5 g
- Carbohydrates 45.5 g
- Sugar 0.3 g
- Protein 9.9 g
- Cholesterol 0 mg

Day 20: Lunch

59-Chicken Tomato Avocado Salad

Total Time: 30 minutes

Serves: 2

Ingredients:
- 6 cups lettuce, chopped
- 2 chicken breasts, boneless and skinless
- 6 oz goat cheese, crumbled
- 1 avocado, halved, seeded and diced
- 1/4 cup basil leaves
- 1 cup cherry tomatoes, halved
- 1 tbsp olive oil
- 1/2 cup balsamic vinegar
- Pepper
- Salt

Directions:
- Heat olive oil in a pan over medium-high heat.

- Place chicken breast in pan and season with pepper and salt.
- Cook chicken for 4 minutes on each side and cut into small pieces.
- In a large bowl, place lettuce leaves and top with goat cheese, chicken, avocado, basil, and tomatoes.
- Pour balsamic vinegar over salad and toss well until combined.
- Serve immediately and enjoy.

Nutritional Value (Amount per Serving):

- Calories 832
- Fat 58.4 g
- Carbohydrates 19.6 g
- Sugar 6.6 g
- Protein 56.5 g
- Cholesterol 157 mg

Day 20: Dinner

60-Creamy Coconut Dill Celery Soup

Total Time: 40 minutes

Serves: 4

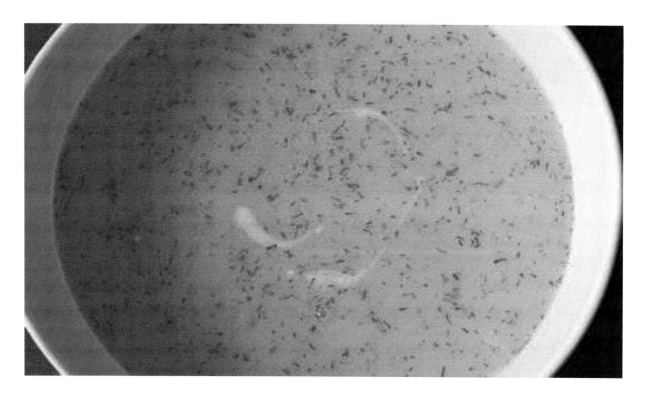

Ingredients:
- 6 cups celery, diced
- 1/2 tsp dill
- 1 medium onion, diced
- 1/2 tsp sea salt
- 2 cups water
- 1 cup coconut milk

Directions:
- Add all ingredients into the saucepan and bring to boil over medium heat.
- Reduce heat to low and simmer for 30 minutes.
- Using blender puree the soup until smooth.
- Stir well and serve.

Nutritional Value (Amount per Serving):

- Calories 174
- Fat 14 g
- Carbohydrates 10 g
- Sugar 5 g
- Protein 2 g
- Cholesterol 0 mg

Day 21: Breakfast

61-Easy Amaranth Breakfast Porridge

Total Time: 25 minutes

Serves: 2

Ingredients:
- 1 cup amaranth
- 2 cups water
- 1 cup coconut milk
- 1/4 tsp salt
- For topping:
- 2 tbsp plain yogurt
- 1 tbsp honey
- 1 cup berries

Directions:
- In a saucepan, add water and coconut milk and bring to boil.
- When water and milk mixture is boil then add amaranth and salt and reduce heat to low and cook for 20 minutes.

- Once amaranth is cooked then pour into the two serving bowls.
- Top with berries, honey, and yogurt.
- Serve immediately and enjoy.

Nutritional Value (Amount per Serving):

- Calories 723
- Fat 35.4 g
- Carbohydrates 89.4 g
- Sugar 20.4 g
- Protein 18.2 g
- Cholesterol 1 mg

Day 21: Lunch

62-Yummy Mixed Fruit Salad

Total Time: 15 minutes

Serves: 10

Ingredients:
- 4 apples, diced
- 4 banana, peeled sliced
- 8 oranges, peeled and segmented
- 4 kiwis, peeled and diced
- 1 cup pomegranate seeds
- 2 tsp poppy seeds
- 3 tbsp fresh lemon juice
- 3 tbsp honey
- 1/4 cup olive oil

Directions:
- In a small bowl, combine together lemon juice, olive oil, poppy seeds and honey.
- In a large bowl, add all fruits and pour lemon juice mixture over the fruits.

- Toss until well coated.
- Serve immediately and enjoy.

Nutritional Value (Amount per Serving):
- Calories 250
- Fat 6.1 g
- Carbohydrates 50.4 g
- Sugar 36.9 g
- Protein 2.7 g
- Cholesterol 0 mg

Day 21: Dinner

63-Easy Grilled Mushrooms

Total Time: 25 minutes

Serves: 4

Ingredients:
- 40 cremini mushrooms
- 8 tbsp olive oil
- 1 tsp sea salt
- 1/2 tsp black pepper

Directions:
- Preheat the oven to 450 F.
- Add mushroom and olive oil in a bowl and toss well.
- Season mushrooms with pepper and salt.
- Place mushrooms on grilled rack in preheated oven for 15 minutes.
- Serve and enjoy.

Nutritional Value (Amount per Serving):

- Calories 295
- Fat 28 g
- Carbohydrates 8 g
- Sugar 3 g
- Protein 5 g
- Cholesterol 0 mg

Day 22: Breakfast

64-Anti-Inflammatory Pineapple Turmeric Smoothie

Total Time: 10 minutes

Serves: 1

Ingredients:
- 1 cup pineapple chunks
- 1/2 banana
- 1 scoop protein powder
- 1/2 tsp turmeric
- 1/2 tsp fresh ginger, grated
- 1 tbsp chia seeds
- 1 cup almond milk, unsweetened

Directions:
- Add all ingredients into the blender and blend until smooth and creamy.
- Pour into the glass and serve.

Nutritional Value (Amount per Serving):

- Calories 969
- Fat 69.2 g
- Carbohydrates 64 g
- Sugar 32.5 g
- Protein 35.6 g
- Cholesterol 65 mg

Day 22: Lunch

65-Roasted Carrots

Total Time: 40 minutes

Serves: 4

Ingredients:
- 16 oz carrots, peeled and cut into 1 1/2 inch pieces
- 3 tbsp honey
- 3 tbsp olive oil
- 1 tbsp thyme
- 2 tbsp parsley, chopped
- 1 tbsp apple cider vinegar
- Pepper
- Salt

Directions:
- Preheat the oven to 400 F.
- Spray a baking tray with cooking spray.

- Place carrots on baking tray and drizzle with olive oil.
- Season with pepper and salt.
- Place the baking tray in preheated oven and bake for 20 minutes.
- In a small bowl, combine together vinegar and honey.
- Drizzle honey and vinegar mixture over the carrots and toss well.
- Again place the baking tray in the oven and bake for 15 minutes.
- After 15 minutes remove baking tray from oven and sprinkle with chopped parsley and thyme. Toss well.
- Serve and enjoy.

Nutritional Value (Amount per Serving):

- Calories 188
- Fat 10.6 g
- Carbohydrates 24.7 g
- Sugar 18.6 g
- Protein 1.1 g
- Cholesterol 0 mg

Day 22: Dinner

66-Parsley Garlic Cauliflower Couscous

Total Time: 30 minutes

Serves: 3

Ingredients:
- 1 medium cauliflower head, cut into florets
- 2 tsp garlic, dried
- 2 tsp parsley, dried
- Pepper
- Salt

Directions:
- Add cauliflower florets into the food processor and process until it looks like couscous.
- Heat large pan over medium-low heat.
- Add cauliflower couscous, parsley, and garlic in the pan and cook until softened.
- Stir well and season with pepper and salt.
- Serve and enjoy.

Nutritional Value (Amount per Serving):

- Calories 51
- Fat 0.2 g
- Carbohydrates 10 g
- Sugar 4 g
- Protein 3 g
- Cholesterol 0 mg

Day 23: Breakfast

67-Quick Quinoa Chia Porridge

Total Time: 10 minutes

Serves: 2

Ingredients:
- 1 tbsp chia seeds
- 2 tsp honey
- 1/2 tsp ground cinnamon
- 1/4 cup walnuts
- 1 cup fresh blueberries
- 2 cups cooked quinoa
- 1 cup cashew milk

Directions:
- In a saucepan, combine together cashew milk and quinoa and heat over medium-low heat.
- Stir in walnuts, cinnamon, and blueberries until evenly warmed.

- Remove saucepan from heat and stir in honey.
- Top with chia seed and serve.

Nutritional Value (Amount per Serving):

- Calories 940
- Fat 29.3 g
- Carbohydrates 139.1 g
- Sugar 18.4 g
- Protein 33.3 g
- Cholesterol 0 mg

Day 23: Lunch

68-Garlic Mustard Chicken

Total Time: 25 minutes

Serves: 4

Ingredients:
- 18 oz chicken breast, boneless and skinless
- 3 garlic cloves, minced
- 2 tbsp olive oil
- 1/4 cup parsley, chopped
- 3 tbsp Dijon mustard
- 4 tbsp honey
- Pepper
- Salt

Directions:
- Heat 1 tbsp olive oil in a pan over medium-high heat and place chicken in the pan.
- Season chicken with pepper and salt and cook for 4 minutes on each side or until cooked.

- Remove chicken from pan and set aside.
- In a small bowl, combine remaining oil, garlic, mustard, and honey.
- Pour honey mixture over the chicken and place chicken again in the pan. Cook for 3 minutes.
- Garnish chicken with chopped parsley.
- Serve hot and enjoy.

Nutritional Value (Amount per Serving):

- Calories 888
- Fat 37.2 g
- Carbohydrates 18.9 g
- Sugar 17.4 g
- Protein 113.3 g
- Cholesterol 338 mg

Day 23: Dinner

69-Baked Potatoes and Broccoli

Total Time: 40 minutes

Serves: 6

Ingredients:
- 4 medium potatoes, cubed
- 1 head broccoli, cut into florets
- 1 tsp seasoning
- 1 tbsp olive oil
- 1 onion, sliced
- 1/2 tsp ground rosemary
- 1/2 tsp garlic powder
- 1/4 tsp pepper

Directions:
- Preheat the oven to 425 F.
- Spray baking dish with cooking spray and set aside.

- Add all ingredients to the bowl and toss well.
- Spread evenly potato mixture on prepared baking dish and bake in preheated oven for 30 minutes.
- Serve hot and enjoy.

Nutritional Value (Amount per Serving):

- Calories 137
- Fat 2.6 g
- Carbohydrates 26.3 g
- Sugar 3 g
- Protein 3.5 g
- Cholesterol 0 mg

Day 24: Breakfast

70-Yummy Chocolate Cherry Shake

Total Time: 10 minutes

Serves: 1

Ingredients:
- 1 tbsp cocoa powder, unsweetened
- 1/2 tsp vanilla extract
- 1 cup almond milk
- 1/2 cup cherries, pitted
- 5 Ice

Directions:
- Add all ingredients into the blender and blend until smooth.
- Serve immediately and enjoy.

Nutritional Value (Amount per Serving):
- Calories 600
- Fat 57.9 g
- Carbohydrates 24.1 g
- Sugar 15.6 g

- Protein 6.5 g
- Cholesterol 0 mg

Day 24: Lunch

71-Creamy Lemon Zucchini Hummus

Total Time: 20 minutes

Serves: 4

Ingredients:
- 4 zucchini, halved
- 1 lemon juice
- 1 tbsp olive oil
- 3 garlic cloves
- 1/4 tsp paprika
- 1/4 cup cilantro, chopped
- 1 tsp cumin
- 3 tbsp tahini
- Pepper
- Salt

Directions:
- Place zucchini on grill and season with pepper and salt.

- Grilled zucchini for 10 minutes.
- Add grilled zucchini, cilantro, cumin, tahini, lemon juice, olive oil, garlic, pepper and salt in a blender and blend until smooth.
- Pour zucchini mixture into a bowl and sprinkle with paprika.
- Serve and enjoy.

Nutritional Value (Amount per Serving):

- Calories 137
- Fat 10.2 g
- Carbohydrates 10.3 g
- Sugar 3.8 g
- Protein 4.6 g
- Cholesterol 0 mg

Day 24: Dinner

72-Walnuts Apple Chicken Salad

Total Time: 25 minutes

Serves: 1

Ingredients:
- 4 oz chicken breasts, skinless and boneless, cooked
- 1 medium apple, cored and diced
- 2 tbsp walnuts, chopped
- 3 tbsp fresh lemon juice
- 3 celery stalk, diced
- 1/8 tsp cinnamon
- Stevia to taste

Directions:
- Cut cooked chicken into the small pieces.
- Add all ingredients to the bowl and toss well until combined.
- Place bowl in refrigerator for 20 minutes.
- Serve chilled and enjoy.

Nutritional Value (Amount per Serving):

- Calories 448
- Fat 18.5 g
- Carbohydrates 35.1 g
- Sugar 25 g
- Protein 37.9 g
- Cholesterol 101 mg

Day 25: Breakfast

73-Walnut Blueberry Yogurt

Total Time: 10 minutes

Serves: 1

Ingredients:
- 1 cup plain yogurt
- 2 tbsp walnuts, chopped
- 3/4 cup fresh blueberries
- 1 cup fresh strawberries

Directions:
- Add all ingredients into the bowl and mix well.
- Serve immediately and enjoy.

Nutritional Value (Amount per Serving):
- Calories 379
- Fat 13 g
- Carbohydrates 45.6 g

- Sugar 35.3 g
- Protein 19.5 g
- Cholesterol 15 mg

Day 25: Lunch

74-Walnut Beet Orange Salad

Total Time: 40 minutes

Serves: 4

Ingredients:
- 1/2 cup walnut
- 3 oranges, peeled and segmented
- 2 large beets, peeled and cut into cubes
- 1/4 cup parsley, chopped
- 2 tbsp apple cider vinegar
- 2 tbsp Dijon mustard
- 3 tbsp orange juice
- 4 tbsp olive oil
- Pepper
- Salt

Directions:
- Take foil piece and place beet on the center of foil. Drizzle with olive oil over the top.

- Wrap and seal aluminum sheet and place in oven at 400 F for 25 minutes.
- In a large bowl, add orange, walnut, parsley, orange juice, olive oil, vinegar and mustard mix well until combined.
- Add roasted beet in bowl and season with pepper and salt.
- Toss well and serve.

Nutritional Value (Amount per Serving):

- Calories 317
- Fat 23.8 g
- Carbohydrates 24.7 g
- Sugar 18.2 g
- Protein 6.4 g
- Cholesterol 0 mg

Day 25: Dinner

75-Simple Chicken Patties

Total Time: 20 minutes

Serves: 4

Ingredients:
- 1 lb ground chicken
- 1/2 tsp ground cumin
- 1 tsp paprika
- 1/2 tsp pepper
- 1/4 tsp red pepper flakes
- 1/2 tsp chili seasoning, no salt added

Directions:
- Preheat the grill.
- Add all ingredients into the large bowl and mix well to combine.
- Make four small round patties from mixture.
- Once the grill is hot then place patties and grill for 5 minutes on each side.
- Serve hot and enjoy.

Nutritional Value (Amount per Serving):

- Calories 220
- Fat 8.6 g
- Carbohydrates 0.8 g
- Sugar 0.1 g
- Protein 33 g
- Cholesterol 101 mg

Day 26: Breakfast

76-Blueberry Breakfast Shake

Total Time: 10 minutes

Serves: 1

Ingredients:
- 3/4 cup almond milk
- 1 tbsp peanut butter
- 1 scoop protein powder
- 1 cup fresh blueberries
- 4 ice

Directions:
- Add all ingredients into the blender and blend until smooth and creamy.
- Serve chilled and enjoy.

Nutritional Value (Amount per Serving):
- Calories 711
- Fat 53.3 g

- Carbohydrates 37.8 g
- Sugar 22.8 g
- Protein 31.4 g
- Cholesterol 65 mg

Day 26: Lunch

77-Simple Marinated Eggplant

Total Time: 2 hours

Serves: 4

Ingredients:
- 18 oz eggplant, cut into slices
- 1 tbsp parsley, chopped
- 1 garlic clove, minced
- 1 small jalapeno pepper, seeded and chopped
- 1 bell pepper, roasted and diced
- 3/4 cup olive oil, divided
- 1/4 tsp pepper
- 1 tsp salt

Directions:
- Place eggplant slices in a dish and sprinkle with salt.
- Brush eggplant slices with oil and set aside for 30 minutes.

- Heat olive oil in a pan over medium-high heat and place eggplant into the pan cook both the side until lightly golden brown.
- Transfer eggplant slices to bowl and add bell pepper, parsley, garlic, jalapeno, pepper, and salt in bowl toss well until combined.
- Cover bowl with lid and place in refrigerator for 1 hour.
- Serve and enjoy.

Nutritional Value (Amount per Serving):

- Calories 368
- Fat 38.1 g
- Carbohydrates 10.4 g
- Sugar 5.5 g
- Protein 1.7 g
- Cholesterol 0 mg

Day 26: Dinner

78-Quick Arugula Almond Peach Salad

Total Time: 15 minutes

Serves: 4

Ingredients:
- 6 cups baby arugula, washed and dried
- 1/2 cup almonds, toasted and sliced
- 3 ripe peaches, pitted and sliced
- 1 tbsp balsamic vinegar
- 1/4 tsp pepper
- 1 tbsp water
- 1 tbsp olive oil
- Pinch of salt

Directions:
- In a large bowl, add arugula, almonds, and peaches. Toss well.
- In a small bowl, combine together water, salt, and vinegar and pour over salad.
- Season with pepper.

- Serve immediately and enjoy.

Nutritional Value (Amount per Serving):

- Calories 152
- Fat 9.9 g
- Carbohydrates 14.3 g
- Sugar 11.6 g
- Protein 4.3 g
- Cholesterol 0 mg

Day 27: Breakfast

79-Mango Turmeric Almond Milk Smoothie

Total Time: 10 minutes

Serves: 1

Ingredients:
- 1/2 cup mango
- 1 tsp coconut oil
- 1/2 tsp turmeric powder
- 1 banana
- 1 cup almond milk, unsweetened
- 1/4 tsp cinnamon
- 1 tsp honey
- 1/2 tsp vanilla extract

Directions:
- Add all ingredients into the blender and blend until smooth.
- Serve and enjoy.

Nutritional Value (Amount per Serving):

- Calories 829
- Fat 62.9 g
- Carbohydrates 72.5 g
- Sugar 51.5 g
- Protein 8.3 g
- Cholesterol 0 mg

Day 27: Lunch

80-Sweet Mango Salsa

Total Time: 15 minutes

Serves: 2

Ingredients:
- 2 cups mango, chopped
- 1 tbsp fresh lemon juice
- 1 garlic clove, minced
- 1/4 cup fresh cilantro, chopped
- 1/2 onion, minced
- Pinch of salt

Directions:
- Add all ingredients to the bowl and toss well.
- Serve and enjoy.

Nutritional Value (Amount per Serving):
- Calories 217

- Fat 1.4 g
- Carbohydrates 53.3 g
- Sugar 47.4 g
- Protein 3.3 g
- Cholesterol 0 mg

Day 27: Dinner

81-Kale Orange Carrot Salad

Total Time: 25 minutes

Serves: 4

Ingredients:
- 8 cups kale, chopped
- 1 carrot, shredded
- 1 fresh orange juice
- 1 tsp orange zest, grated
- 1/8 tsp red chili flakes
- 1/4 tsp ground cumin
- 1 red bell pepper, diced
- 2 garlic cloves, minced
- 1 onion, diced
- 2 tsp olive oil
- Pepper

Directions:

- Heat olive oil in a large pan over medium heat.
- Add onion to the pan and sauté for 2 minutes.
- Add kale, bell pepper, garlic and orange juice and stir well.
- Reduce heat to medium-low and cook for another 5 minutes.
- Add remaining ingredients and stir well.
- Cover pan with lid and cook for another 5 minutes.
- Serve and enjoy.

Nutritional Value (Amount per Serving):

- Calories 126
- Fat 2.5 g
- Carbohydrates 23.3 g
- Sugar 5.2 g
- Protein 5 g
- Cholesterol 0 mg

Day 28: Breakfast

82-Cauliflower Apple Coconut Porridge

Total Time: 10 minutes

Serves: 2

Ingredients:
- 1 apple, peeled and chopped
- 1/2 cup coconut milk
- 10 oz cauliflower, cut into florets
- 1/4 tsp cinnamon

Directions:
- Steam cauliflower florets until soften.
- Add steamed cauliflower, coconut milk, cinnamon, and apple into the blender and blend until smooth.
- Serve and enjoy.

Nutritional Value (Amount per Serving):
- Calories 232

- Fat 14.6 g
- Carbohydrates 26.5 g
- Sugar 17 g
- Protein 4.5 g
- Cholesterol 0 mg

Day 28: Lunch

83-Spinach Mushroom Egg Scramble

Total Time: 20 minutes

Serves: 2

Ingredients:
- 3 organic eggs, lightly beaten
- 1/4 cup bell peppers, chopped
- 4 mushrooms, chopped
- 1 tbsp coconut oil
- 1/2 cup spinach, chopped
- Pepper
- Salt

Directions:
- Heat 1/2 tablespoon of coconut oil in a pan over medium heat.
- Add chopped vegetables in a pan and sauté for 5 minutes.
- Heat remaining coconut oil in another pan.
- Once the oil is hot then add eggs and cook over medium heat. Stir frequently.

- Season cooked eggs with pepper and salt.
- Add sautéed vegetables in egg and stir well.
- Serve and enjoy.

Nutritional Value (Amount per Serving):

- Calories 167
- Fat 13.5 g
- Carbohydrates 3.1 g
- Sugar 1.9 g
- Protein 9.8 g
- Cholesterol 246 mg

Day 28: Dinner

84-Artichoke Avocado Spinach Salad

Total Time: 15 minutes

Serves: 4

Ingredients:
- 14 oz artichoke hearts, drained and halved
- 1 avocado, peeled and diced
- 4 cups fresh spinach, clean and torn
- 1/2 cup scallions, chopped
- 1/2 tsp garlic, minced
- 4 tbsp fresh lemon juice
- 1/4 tsp pepper

Directions:
- In a mixing bowl, add spinach, scallions, avocado, and artichoke and toss well.
- In a small bowl, combine together lemon juice, garlic, and pepper and pour over salad. Toss well.
- Serve immediately and enjoy.

Nutritional Value (Amount per Serving):

- Calories 165
- Fat 10.2 g
- Carbohydrates 17.3 g
- Sugar 2 g
- Protein 5.4 g
- Cholesterol 0 mg

Day 29: Breakfast

85-Quick Creamy Banana Oatmeal

Total Time: 10 minutes

Serves: 1

Ingredients:
- 1 medium banana
- 1/4 tsp cinnamon
- 2 tbsp coconut butter
- Pinch of salt

Directions:
- Add banana, cinnamon, and salt in a blender and blend until smooth.
- Heat coconut butter in a saucepan over low heat.
- Once it warm then remove from heat and add banana mixture into the pan and stir well.
- Serve immediately and enjoy.

Nutritional Value (Amount per Serving):
- Calories 478
- Fat 36.4 g
- Carbohydrates 41.4 g

- Sugar 18.3 g
- Protein 5.3 g
- Cholesterol 0 mg

Day 29: Lunch

86-Easy Egg Tomato Scramble

Total Time: 15 minutes

Serves: 2

Ingredients:
- 6 organic eggs, lightly beaten
- 15 oz tomatoes, diced
- 1 tbsp coconut oil
- 2 tbsp fresh parsley, chopped
- Pepper
- Salt

Directions:
- Heat oil in a pan over medium heat.
- Once the oil is hot then add tomatoes and cook for 4 minutes.
- Add beaten eggs and stir until eggs are cooked.
- Add parsley and stir well to mix.
- Season with pepper and salt.

- Serve and enjoy.

Nutritional Value (Amount per Serving):

- Calories 287
- Fat 20.4 g
- Carbohydrates 9.6 g
- Sugar 6.6 g
- Protein 18.6 g
- Cholesterol 491 mg

Day 29: Dinner

87-Roasted Rosemary Orange Chicken

Total Time: 45 minutes

Serves: 4

Ingredients:

- 16 oz chicken breasts, skinless
- 1 tsp rosemary, chopped
- 1 garlic clove, chopped
- 1/4 cup orange juice
- 1/2 tsp olive oil
- Pepper

Directions:

- Preheat the oven to 450 F.
- Spray a baking tray with cooking spray and set aside.
- Rub garlic and olive oil over the chicken.
- Season chicken with rosemary and pepper.
- Place seasoned chicken in the prepared baking tray.

- Pour orange juice over the chicken and bake in preheated oven for 25 minutes.
- Flip the chicken to other side and bake for another 10 minutes.
- Serve and enjoy.

Nutritional Value (Amount per Serving):

- Calories 230
- Fat 9.1 g
- Carbohydrates 2.1 g
- Sugar 1.3 g
- Protein 33 g
- Cholesterol 101 mg

Day 30: Breakfast

88-Cinnamon Carrot Banana Smoothie

Total Time: 10 minutes

Serves: 1

Ingredients:
- 1/2 carrot, chopped
- 1/2 cup coconut milk
- 1/2 tbsp coconut oil
- 1 banana
- 1 apple, chopped
- 1/4 tsp cinnamon
- 1 cup ice

Directions:
- Add all ingredients into the blender and blend until smooth and creamy.
- Pour into the glass and serve.

Nutritional Value (Amount per Serving):

- Calories 570
- Fat 36.2 g
- Carbohydrates 67.9 g
- Sugar 43.2 g
- Protein 4.9 g
- Cholesterol 0 mg

Day 30: Lunch

89-Delicious Tomato Cauliflower Rice

Total Time: 20 minutes

Serves: 3

Ingredients:
- 1 cauliflower head, cut into florets
- 3 garlic cloves, minced
- 1/2 cup onion, diced
- 1 tbsp olive oil
- 1/4 cup vegetable broth
- 2 tbsp tomato paste
- 1 tsp cumin
- 1 tsp salt

Directions:
- Add cauliflower florets in food processor and process until it looks like rice.
- Heat large pan over medium heat.
- Add onion to the pan and sauté for 3 minutes.

- Add minced garlic and sauté for 30 seconds.
- Add cauliflower rice, cumin, and salt and stir well until combined.
- Add tomato paste and broth and stir until tomato paste dissolves completely.
- Serve warm and enjoy.

Nutritional Value (Amount per Serving):

- Calories 89
- Fat 5.1 g
- Carbohydrates 9.9 g
- Sugar 4.3 g
- Protein 3.1 g
- Cholesterol 0 mg

Day 30: Dinner

90-Baked Mustard Salmon

Total Time: 25 minutes

Serves: 4

Ingredients:
- 1 lb salmon, slice into 4 fillets
- 1 fresh lemon juice
- 2 tbsp dill, chopped
- 2 tbsp mustard

Directions:
- Preheat the oven to 450 F.
- Place salmon fillets on a baking tray.
- Add all remaining ingredients into the bowl and brush over the salmon fillets.
- Bake in preheated oven for 15 minutes.
- Serve warm and enjoy.

Nutritional Value (Amount per Serving):
- Calories 183
- Fat 8.8 g

- Carbohydrates 3.1 g
- Sugar 0.6 g
- Protein 23.8 g
- Cholesterol 50 mg

Conversion Chart

100 °F	37.78 °C
110 °F	43.33 °C
120 °F	48.89 °C
130 °F	54.44 °C
140 °F	60.00 °C
150 °F	65.56 °C
160 °F	71.11 °C
170 °F	76.67 °C
180 °F	82.22 °C
190 °F	87.78 °C
200 °F	93.33 °C
300 °F	148.89 °C
400 °F	204.44 °C
500 °F	260.00 °C

Made in the USA
Middletown, DE
06 October 2017